St Anne's: The Story of a Guinness Estate

Joan Ussher Sharkey

Ardilaun coat of arms and motto, *Spes Mea in Deo* – My hope is in God. *Gillman collection*.

St Anne's:
The Story of a Guinness Estate

Joan Ussher Sharkey

The Woodfield Press
in association with
Dublin City Council

This book was typeset by
Red Barn Publishing, Skeagh, Co. Cork for
THE WOODFIELD PRESS
17 Jamestown Square, Dublin 8
www.woodfield-press.com
e-mail: terri.mcdonnell@ireland.com

Publishing Editor
Helen Harnett

House Editor
Aidan Culhane

© The Woodfield Press and Joan Ussher Sharkey 2002

A catalogue record for this title
is available from the British Library.

ISBN 0-9534293-4-2

All rights reserved. No part of this publication may be reproduced or transmitted in any form or by any means, including photocopying and recording, without written permission of the publisher and the author. Such written permission must also be obtained before any part of this publication is stored in a retrieval system of any nature.

Printed in Ireland
by ColourBooks, Dublin

Dedication

In memory of my late Mum, Christina McArdle,
from Ballybough, Dublin,
my *anam cara*,
and my Dad, Joseph Ussher,
from Wood Quay, Galway,
who unknowingly
sparked my interest in family and local history

Also published by The Woodfield Press

The Wicklow World of Elizabeth Smith (1840–1850)
DERMOT JAMES and SÉAMAS Ó MAITIÚ, Editors

The Sligo-Leitrim World of Kate Cullen (1832–1913)
revealed by HILARY PYLE

Ballyknockan: A Wicklow Stonecutters' Village
SÉAMAS Ó MAITIÚ and BARRY O'REILLY

The Tellicherry Five: The Transportation of Michael Dwyer and the Wicklow Rebels
KIERAN SHEEDY

John Hamilton of Donegal 1800–1884: This Recklessly Generous Landlord
DERMOT JAMES

Red-Headed Rebel: A Biography of Susan Mitchell
HILARY PYLE

Charles Dickens' Ireland: An Anthology
JIM COOKE

*Faith or Fatherhood? Bishop Dunboyne's Dilemma –
The Story of John Butler, Catholic Bishop of Cork 1763–1787*
CON COSTELLO

W & R Jacob: Celebrating 150 Years of Irish Biscuit Making
SÉAMAS Ó MAITIÚ

Female Activists: Irish Women and Change (1900–1960)
MARY CULLEN and MARIA LUDDY, Editors

The Politics and Relationships of Kathleen Lynn
MARIE MULHOLLAND

CONTENTS

Acknowlegements		ix
Foreword		xi
Chronology		xiii
Introduction		xv
Chapter One	Clontarf and Raheny in the Early Nineteenth Century	1
Chapter Two	The Guinness Family	5
Chapter Three	The Origin of St Anne's House and Estate	9
Chapter Four	Development of the Estate and Gardens	17
Chapter Five	The Ascending Years	24
Chapter Six	Major Expansions	31
Chapter Seven	Acquisitions: 1874–1875	34
Chapter Eight	Acquisitions: 1876–1878	43
Chapter Nine	House, Grounds and New Buildings	46
Chapter Ten	More Land Dealings	57
Chapter Eleven	The Twilight Years	68
Chapter Twelve	Dublin Corporation Years	79
Notes		98
Bibliography		106
Index		111

Lady Ardilaun, 'tall, dark, very upright, good-looking, with charming, expressive grey eyes, and dignified in a manner that was slightly alarming'.
Katherine Everett, *Brick and Flowers,* p.156.
Courtesy of the National Library of Ireland R 27818.

Acknowledgements

There are many people who have assisted me in the publication of this book. Firstly, my thanks to Gerry Barry, Superintendent of the Parks and Landscape Services of Dublin City Council for his financial support for the book and his interest and help in many ways since I first approached him four years ago. Terese McMullin, Muniments Section, Law Department allowed me to research all the legal documents and correspondence relating to the St. Anne's Compulsory Purchase Order. Mary Clarke and her staff in the City Archives gave me time and space to do the research, and organised photography of the original deed maps by David Davison. Leo Collins and Peggy Kearns from Survey and Mapping Section updated the present map of St Anne's Park at great speed. All the photographs collected by the former Assistant Parks Superintendent, Maryann Harris, were made available to me, as well as other photographs in the Parks files. Martin McChree took recent photographs of the park and Rob Goodbody located other photographs for me.

Charles Plunket has been very helpful in answering all my queries over the years and has shown great interest in the publication of the book. He has been most generous in making copies from his collection of photographs of St. Anne's estate available to be used in this publication. My thanks also to Daniel Gillman for giving me permission to use photographs from his large collection.

I am grateful to all my fellow members in the Raheny Heritage Society who have encouraged and supported me in many ways. The Society also made their photographs available for me to use. In particular I would like to thank Kathleen O'Connor for her constant advice and guidance and also for suggesting the title of the book. Niall McDevitt lightened the burden for me by working on the Guinness and Plunket Family Tree. Mary Dunne and Frank Pelly also gave assistance.

Douglas Appleyard gave me a vital piece of information which greatly added to the history of the Thornhill estate. Eibhlin Roche, the Guinness archivist, answered all my queries efficiently and promptly. Seamus Kearns allowed me to reproduce postcards from his collection. Myrtle Allan permitted me to use the copy of the Henry Hill sketch of St Ann's.

The staff in the Irish Architectural Archives, National Library, National Archives, Registry of Deeds, Valuation Office, and the Gilbert Library were attentive and helpful. My thanks to Leo Devitt for lending me photographs and his tracing of the mansion survey. OS Maps have been reproduced from the Ordnance Survey Ireland Permit No. MP 003602. © Ordnance Survey Ireland and Government of Ireland.

The many informative discussions with Arthur Garrett on the local history of the area were much appreciated. Molly Milne shared details of her own family history at Maryville house with me. The Golfing Society of Ireland kindly lent me their copy of the *Royal Dublin Golf Club, 1885–1985, Centenary*. A last-minute call for help to Éanna Brophy was answered generously and eloquently.

Thanks to Aidan Culhane for editing my manuscript, Brendan Lyons for typesetting and Mark Loughran for designing the cover. The expert advice and encouragement given by Terri McDonnell of The Woodfield Press was an enormous help all along the way.

Last but not least, my husband Des, my sons Colm and Cillian, and my brother Bernard, gave endless back up support during all this period.

Joan Ussher Sharkey

FOREWORD

The Guinness family's contribution to the City of Dublin has been immense and nowhere is this more apparent than in the Clontarf/Raheny area where the family developed St Anne's estate. With its magnificent avenue of Holm Oaks and Austrian Pines, its Clock Tower, Red Stables, its woodlands, lake and follies, all represented over 100 years of endeavour up until the late 1930s when Dublin Corporation acquired the estate.

It is only natural that one of Dublin's wealthiest families would develop a prestigious estate such as St Anne's as its home and it is likely that some horticultural competitiveness existed with nearby properties such as Howth demesne and Malahide Castle.

The recent history of St Anne's is well known by local people and its development as an outstanding regional park serving the north Dublin City area in particular is widely acknowledged. However, the development of the original St Anne's estate by the Guinness family from the 1830s onwards is a story worth telling. The author Joan Ussher Sharkey has had a life long interest in St Anne's and the Guinness connection. As a resident of Raheny, and given her involvement with the Raheny Heritage Society, she is well placed to tell the story of St Anne's and her book is a culmination of many years of research and endeavour.

Dublin City Council is pleased to support this publication and recognises it as a valuable contribution to the history of our premier city park and its adjoining localities.

Gerard Barry
City Parks Superintendent
Dublin City Council
June 2002

CHRONOLOGY

1747	John Vernon of Clontarf Castle leases 29 Irish acres at Blackbush, Clontarf to Paul Hale and his brothers for a term of 99 years
1796	Margaret Holmes, only child of Paul Hale, assigns the Blackbush land to her son John Holmes
1814	Thornhill House built on the Blackbush land by Sergeant John Ball
1829	Hugh and Fleming O'Reilly, solicitors, living at Thornhill; John Holmes puts the land in trust to William Jameson and William Mulock
1835	Brothers Arthur Lee and Benjamin Lee Guinness buy the lease of Thornhill estate from O'Reilly family and trustees of Holmes family; new leases signed with John Vernon
1836	Guinness brothers lease 36 acres of land in Raheny from Ellen Ball
1837	Benjamin Lee marries his first cousin Elizabeth Guinness and builds a new house, called St Ann's after the nearby holy well
1838	Arthur Lee sells his share in St Ann's to his brother Benjamin Lee
1839	Tower bridge is built to commemorate the birth of Anne Lee Guinness
1850	Benjamin Lee signs new lease for 23 acres in Raheny with the Earl of Howth and loses remainder of land to Patrick Boland
1852	Benjamin Lee buys Ashford estate and land in Co. Mayo and Co. Galway
1854	Bedford Lodge and land in Clontarf is added to St Anne's estate
1856	Benjamin Lee buys new town house, 80/81 St Stephen's Green
1867	Benjamin Lee is granted a baronetcy, first title in Guinness family
1868	Sir Benjamin Lee dies leaving an estate valued at one million pounds; Sir Arthur Edward (eldest son) inherits St Anne's and Ashford estates
1871	Sir Arthur marries Lady Olive White, daughter of the Earl of Bantry
1872	The future right of presentation to Raheny Church of Ireland parish is vested in Sir Arthur and his heirs
1873	Work on remodelling St Anne's house starts
1874	Signs new lease for Bedford Lodge with 27 acres of other land nearby; major expansion of estate by new lease of 277 acres of Raheny land
1876	Sybil Hill estate is added to St Anne's; Sir Arthur retires from partnership of brewery with large settlement
1878	Maryville estate is added to St Anne's, which now totals under 500 acres
1880	Sir Arthur buys land at St Stephen's Green and opens it as public park; elevated to peerage, becomes Lord Ardilaun
1885	Building of new Stables commences
1889	New church called All Saints' is opened on the estate
1891	Lord Ardilaun leases 2 acres of North Bull Island from Earl of Howth
1894	Lord Ardilaun buys remainder of North Bull Island in Raheny parish
1898	Acquires lease of Baymount Castle and later opens Baymount School
1900	Clontarf and Hill of Howth Company acquires two acres along St Anne's estate and new tramline opens; Queen Victoria visits St Anne's

1902	North Bull Island and foreshore in Clontarf Parish bought from Landed Estates Court, subject to lease of 1892 to Royal Dublin Golf Club
1915	Lord Ardilaun dies and is buried in All Saints' Church Raheny; auction of livestock and crops and letting of farm land to yearly tenants
1916	Katherine Everett comes to live in Sybil Hill as companion and secretary to Lady Ardilaun; long leases for houses on estate are given to tenants
1925	Lady Ardilaun dies and is buried along her husband in All Saints' Church; St Anne's estate inherited by Benjamin Plunket, Bishop of Meath, and nephew of Lord Ardilaun
1932	Bishop Plunket puts the estate on the market
1933	Wedding reception of Olive Plunket, daughter of Bishop Plunket, to Viscount Milton, heir of Lord Fitzwilliam, is held in St Anne's
1934	Bishop Plunket buys the freehold of 47 acres around St Anne's house
1936	Dublin Corporation in discussions with Bishop Plunket to acquire St Anne's estate
1938	Right of presentation of rector to All Saints' Church is relinquished by Bishop Plunket and church transferred to Representative Church Body
1939	St Anne's Compulsory Purchase Order is confirmed; Bishop Plunket moves to Sybil Hill; fine art auction is held in St Anne's house
1943	Fire destroys St Anne's house, only walls remain
1947	Bishop Plunket dies and is buried in grounds of All Saints' Church; Sybil Hill inherited by his son Benjamin.
1950	Sybil Hill is sold to Vincentian Fathers and St Paul's College opens
1952	Building of new housing estate at St Anne's; tree-lined avenues retained as a public park; land exchange between Dublin Corporation and Vincentians; Sybil Hill Road opens connecting Clontarf and Raheny
1959	Maryville is sold to Vincentians; house demolished, land used as playing fields for school
1968	Shell of St Anne's house is demolished
1975	Rose Garden opens
1978	Bedford Lodge becomes the headquarters of the Parks Department
1981	International Rose Trials starts
1988	Millinnium Arboretum opens
1995	Parks Department moves into new Civic Offices; Bedford Lodge is sold

Introduction

The north coast of Dublin Bay stretches from Clontarf to Howth Head and the area today offers the public an abundant choice of open green spaces with many recreational facilities, all within easy distance of the capital city. First there is the natural amenity of the sea itself, with lovely views stretching from Howth Head across the bay to the Dublin and Wicklow Mountains. The wild beauty of the cliff walks and heath-covered hills of Howth Head have been enjoyed by Dubliners for years, while the gardens and grounds of Howth Castle are today open to the public and offer many attractions, including three public golf courses. The recent confirmation of Howth as a Special Amenity Area will protect its natural environment for generations to come. The Clontarf Promenade is also a favourite place for everyone to stroll, while the more energetic can use the cycle path from Raheny to Sutton, all close to the seashore.

Another Special Amenity Area is situated nearby on North Bull Island. At present this island is five kilometres long and one kilometre wide, and runs parallel to the coastline from Clontarf to Sutton. The island is of national and international importance, but is of relatively recent origin, having been only a small sand bar in 1800 and reached its present length by 1902. The formation of the island was due largely to the construction of the South Wall, known as 'The Piles', in 1730 and of the North Bull Wall much later in 1824. For years, the accumulation of silt in the bay made navigation into Dublin Port difficult and constant dredging was required. The construction of the two great walls combined with the scouring action of the tides formed a deep channel into the port. As a result, sediment began to accumulate outside the North Bull Wall, resulting in the growth of the island. It is still growing today, but mainly in width rather than length.

North Bull Island was declared a bird sanctuary in 1931, a UNESCO Biosphere Reserve in 1981, a nature reserve in 1988, and a Special Amenity Area in 1994. In 1955, Dublin Corporation bought the whole island except the area owned by the Royal Dublin Golf Club. The other golf club on the island, St Anne's, is leased from Dublin Corporation. North Bull Island is home to thousands of birds and numerous wild plants, and along with Dollymount Beach has been enjoyed and utilised by birdwatchers, children, adults and the general public for years. It is the biggest public park maintained by the Parks and Landscape Services Division of Dublin City Council (formerly Dublin Corporation).

The next biggest park under its management is situated directly opposite North Bull Island, straddling the two modern Dublin suburbs of Clontarf and Raheny. This is St Anne's Regional Park, covering 305 acres and providing the public with a wide range of facilities, including football pitches, tennis courts, a 12-hole par-three golf course, a children's play area, a model car track, an arboretum, a green waste recycling facility, as well as the renowned Rose Garden, which has become a centre for yearly international rose trials.[1] In our busy modern life, St Anne's also provides an air of tranquility with its distinctive evergreen trees woven through with woodland paths.

St Anne's owes its origin to the Guinness brewing family, who acquired a house and a small estate of 50 acres in Clontarf in 1835 that became their family home. This book tells the story of how the Guinness family acquired the estate, expanding it over the years into a beautiful demesne of almost 500 acres, and traces the development of the estate to the present day.

CHAPTER ONE

Clontarf and Raheny in the Early Nineteenth Century

The northern suburbs of Dublin were slow to develop. Up to and including much of the eighteenth century, the shoreline ran from the Clontarf coastline to Ballybough and along the present North Strand. The only access to the northeast area of the city was over the Tolka River at Ballybough Bridge. The construction of Annesley Bridge in 1797 offered another route and helped to open up the area. Clontarf, although it was only two and a half miles from the city centre, had formerly been a fishing village. Even in the early nineteenth century, some of the old 'Clontarf Sheds', wooden buildings used for curing fish at the edge of the sea, still remained. But changes were coming and in the 1830s Clontarf was also becoming a popular bathing place, much frequented by Dubliners, with lodging houses being built along the coast road; inland there were numerous pleasant villas and cottages.[1] Among these was a house called Thornhill, which was at that time occupied by Fleming and Hugh O'Reilly, solicitors who also had a town house at 15 Mountjoy Square North. This was the house that the Guinness family acquired in Clontarf.

The neighbouring parish of Raheny was situated four and a half miles from Dublin on the road to Howth and was bounded on the east by the sea, with most of the land in meadow and pasture, and arable land producing excellent crops of wheat.[2] Raheny parish was very rural and according to the 1831 census covered an area of 920 acres. The total population of the parish was only 608, of whom 282 lived in the village. On the other hand, Clontarf parish, although only slightly bigger in area (1190 acres), was much more developed, with a larger population of 3,323, of whom 1,309 lived in the town of Clontarf.

The two major landlords on the northside of Dublin Bay at the beginning of the nineteenth century were the Vernon family of Clontarf Castle and the St Lawrence family of Howth Castle. The residence and tenure of Howth Castle began at the time of the Anglo-Norman settlement, and it has continued without interruption for over 800 years, which must be rather unique in Ireland. In 1177, Almeric Tristram, brother-in-law and companion in arms to Sir John de Courcey, a Norman knight, landed at Howth and won a battle against the Danes, for which service he was rewarded with the grant of lands at Howth. The battle was fought on the feast of St Lawrence, and it has been suggested that he thus adopted the name as his family surname.[3] In 1188, Nicholas, son of Almeric Tristram, executed a deed confirming the Howth lands to his son, also called Almeric, who was granted a royal confirmation of the lands sometime before 1190 by the future King John, then Lord of Ireland.[4]

A great portion of the Raheny lands belonged to the priory of the Holy Trinity in Dublin, i.e. Christ Church, while King Henry II confirmed other lands in Raheny to St Mary's Abbey. In 1189 Pope Clement III confirmed to St Mary's Abbey the grant of their possessions, which King John further renewed, describing the premises as 'the lands of Ratheny with the chapel, etc.' Later the priory of Christ Church exchanged the main part of their estates in Raheny with St Mary's Abbey for other possessions. A section of Raheny was about the same time granted by Earl Strongbow to John de Courcey, who set out from Raheny to conquer Ulster. Later, after de Courcey had been put down, the de Lacy Family were Lords of Raheny for a time, but the rivalry between the these two families forced King John to come to Ireland to restore peace and banish the de Lacys in 1211. At the dissolution of the religious houses in the sixteenth century, St Mary's Abbey still held 30 acres of land as well as the rectory of Raheny, and about this time the St Lawrence family acquired their title in the locality.[5] It is difficult to unravel the actual sequence of land ownership by the St Lawrence family in Raheny over the following years. The first record of the family in the Raheny area is from 1572, when Christopher, the 'blind lord' of Howth, built a dower house in Raheny, called St Lawrence Hall, which bore a tablet with the coats of arms of the St Lawrence family and that of his wife Elizabeth Plunkett. This tablet was only removed to Howth Castle in 1910.[6] In 1606 Nicholas, Lord Howth died in possession of 60 acres in Raheny, but by 1654 the Civil Survey records Lord Howth in possession of 340 acres as his inheritance, while the total area of Raheny parish amounted to 479 acres.[7] By 1831 Lord Howth was recorded as the main owner in fee of the parish of Raheny,[8] and his descendants held these lands right up to the middle of the twentieth century.

Clontarf is celebrated in Irish history as the scene of the famous battle in 1014, which put an end to the Danish power in Dublin. After the Norman invasion, Hugh de Lacy granted Clontarf to Adam de Phepoe. Later, in 1172, King Henry II granted Clontarf to the Knights Templar, but in 1312, when the order was dissolved by Pope Clement, its lands were transferred to another order, the Knights Hospitallers at Kilmainham, who administered Clontarf Church and Manor until the Reformation.[9] John Vernon was the quartermaster general of Cromwell's army in Ireland in 1640. Cromwell granted the confiscated Clontarf estate to Captain John Blackwell, and later John Vernon acquired the lands from him and thus established the Vernon family in Clontarf for almost 300 years.[10] The Names Books of the Ordnance Survey in 1837 records that the civil parish of Clontarf was then the property of Mr John Edward Venables Vernon, who was also lord of the manor with the right to hold manor courts, although these had not been held for many years. The survey also states that work was still in progress on the building of John Vernon's new mansion at Clontarf. Apparently the old Norman castle, which had been added to over the years, was in danger of collapsing; a new castle, designed by William Morison, was begun in 1835, the same year that the Guinness family leased the estate and house called Thornhill from John Vernon.

The Thornhill house and land were situated in the townland known as Blackbush or Heronstown, in the civil parish of Clontarf. It had a splendid situation: beside the sea, on a natural height, overlooking Dublin Bay, with views stretching from Howth Head to the Dublin and Wicklow Mountains. The Naniken River was the northern boundary of the property, and was also the boundary between the civil parishes of Clontarf and Raheny. From this small beginning would grow a large estate carved out of the landholdings of both the Vernon and St Lawrence families over the next 100 years, bought and maintained by the wealth of the Guinness family.

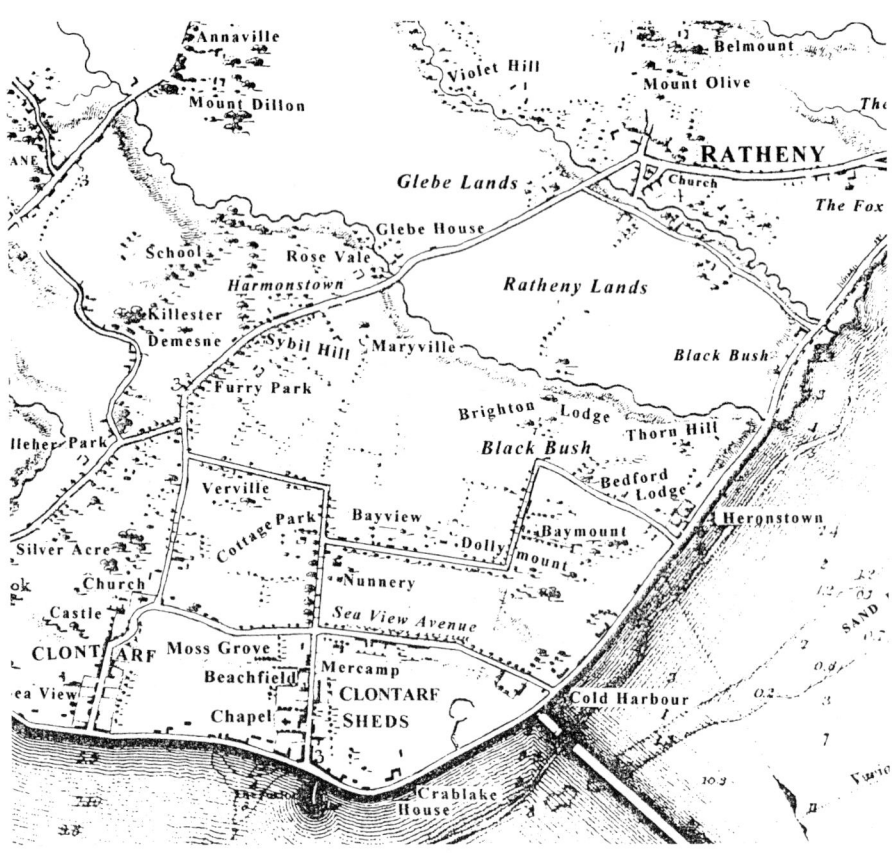

Duncan's Map of Dublin, 1821, showing Clontarf/Raheny area and Thornhill house.

CHAPTER TWO

The Guinness Family

To appreciate the development of St Anne's, one must look briefly at the origin of the family who came to live there. The fortune of the Guinness family came from the sale of a dark brown beer, which was brewed towards the end of the eighteenth century at St James's Gate, Dublin. The brewery was situated on the River Liffey, which would in the years ahead become a 'river of gold' for the family. Frederic Mullally described it in his book on the Guinness family, *The Silver Salver*.

The first Arthur Guinness was born in 1725, the eldest son of Richard Guinness and Elizabeth Read. Richard was land agent and receiver to the Reverend Dr Arthur Price, Rector of the Church of Ireland parish of Celbridge, Co Kildare, who later became Archbishop of Cashel. Dr Price built Celbridge House, later known as Oakley Park. Part of Richard Guinness's duties was to brew ale for the workers on the Archbishop's estate. Dr Price also acquired James Carberry's Brewery in Celbridge, which was managed by his agent and was probably the first home of the Guinness family in Celbridge.[1] Richard's first son, Arthur, was named after the Archbishop and was his godson. When Dr Price died in 1752, he left £100 to his agent Richard, who invested his legacy in a coaching inn in Celbridge, which he ran for many years with his second wife, Elizabeth Clare. Dr Price also left £100 in his will to his godson, Arthur, who leased a small brewery with this bequest at Leixlip in 1756, and thus began his career as a brewer. After three years, Arthur had built up a successful business and, leaving his brother Richard to run the brewery in Leixlip, he turned his attention to Dublin City to further his business career.[2]

At that time brewing was one of Dublin's principal industries, but brewing failures were also common and only the efficient survived.

Success in the brewing industry was acceptable to society, and by the end of the century it was an occupation consistent with high social position. With thoughts of furthering his business prospects, young Arthur's eye fell on a run-down brewery at James's Gate, west of the city centre. The property was owned by the Rainsford family and had been leased to Paul Espinasse in 1715. The property, which Arthur acquired in 1759, was large and included a commodious dwelling house and garden; but the brewery itself was small and poorly equipped and had not been used for some years. It had a frontage of 89 feet (27 metres) onto James's Street and extended southward almost 400 feet (122 metres) to Rainsford Street. Most importantly, it was adjacent to the city watercourse. Arthur obtained the lease of this brewery for a term of 9,000 years at a rent of £45 per year.[3] He devoted his time and energy to turning the James's Gate brewery into a thriving business.

Another event that contributed to his prosperity and helped his social standing was his marriage to Olivia Whitmore, an heiress with impressive family connections both in business and political circles, in 1761. Two years later he was elected Warden of the Dublin Corporation of Brewers. Within a few short years of starting the James's Gate brewery, Arthur had become a very successful businessman and could afford to live in the style of a gentleman. By 1764, he had bought a country house at Beaumont, Co. Dublin, which today is a nursing home called Beaumont Convalescent Home, run by the Sisters of Charity. After 20 years in business, Arthur had become brewer to Dublin Castle and had also built flourmills at Kilmainham. He became active in public life, becoming Governor of the Meath Hospital as well as financially supporting repairs to St Patrick's Cathedral. He founded Ireland's first Sunday School in 1785, and also took a keen interest in his local parish of Coolock, beside his Beaumont home. Arthur and his wife Olivia had 21 children but only 10 survived infancy. Arthur died in 1803, at the age of 78, and was laid to rest in the churchyard at Oughterard, Co. Kildare alongside his parents. At his death, the brewery was the biggest employer in Dublin and he left an estate valued at around £25,000, which by any standard was prosperous.[4]

The second Arthur Guinness was born on 12 March 1768 at St James's Gate, the third child and the second son of the first Arthur. The eldest son, Hosea, had became a clergyman in the Church of Ireland and was Rector of St Werburgh's in Dublin until his death in 1841. The second Arthur was destined to become the brewer in the family. His father bequeathed to him the silver salver that had been presented to him by the Corporation of Brewers of the City of Dublin. He stated in the will that it was to be given to 'the eldest male branch of my family then living who shall be in the brewing trade', and since then it has been handed down through the generations. It was still held by the third Lord Iveagh at the time of his death in June 1992, and he was the last member of the Guinness family to head the brewing company. The second Arthur married Anne Lee in 1793, daughter of Benjamin Lee of Merrion, and they had nine children. His younger brother Benjamin, who also worked in the brewery, married Anne Lee's sister, Rebecca, thus perpetuating the middle name 'Lee' in later generations of the brewing branch of the family. The second Arthur became in fact the head of the family. He was also uncle to a large number of nephews and nieces, three of whom married his own children. He took his responsibility as head of the family very seriously and even financially baled out many of his relatives who fell by the wayside and didn't live up to his own high standards as a businessman and an evangelical Christian.[5]

In business, the second Arthur was shrewd, forthright and immensely able, becoming his father's partner when he was 30. Besides brewing, banking was his principal business interest, and he became a director of the Bank of Ireland and eventually Governor in 1820. His excellent business skills were sought by his fellow citizens and he held many public offices, including serving on the Dublin Ballast Board, Dublin Chamber of Commerce and the Meath Hospital, to name but a few.[6] Initially trade at the James's Gate brewery was mainly in the Dublin area. Under the second Arthur's administration, trade to the rest of Ireland was opened up and within his lifetime output reached over three million gallons (13.5 million litres), of which exports to England and Scotland represented a large proportion. By 1837, Guinness porter was well established in London as a quality drink. It is recorded that one wounded officer at the Battle of Waterloo in 1815 attributed his recovery to drinking Guinness.[7] By the latter part of the 1830s, when he was almost 70 years of age, Arthur had transferred much of the burden of the day-to-day administration to his two sons, Arthur Lee and Benjamin Lee, and also to John Purser Jnr, a London master brewer. And it is with these two brothers, and particularly Benjamin Lee, that the history of St Anne's begins in 1835.

Benjamin Lee Guinness (1798–1868). *Drawing by W.A. Wragg, Courtesy of the National Library of Ireland.*

CHAPTER THREE

The Origin of St Anne's House and Estate

By the year 1835, the brothers Arthur Lee and Benjamin Lee were both prosperous single young men, in their thirties. They were living in the town house adjacent to the brewery at number 1 Thomas Street, but were looking for a country house of their own, as would befit their social and business standing. They found their house, Thornhill, in Clontarf. As mentioned previously, Thornhill was at this time occupied by the O'Reilly family. To acquire the property the Guinness brothers had to buy out the interest of all the people who held leases on the property.

The first record of this property was a lease dated 16 May 1747. John Vernon of Clontarf Castle granted the Blackbush land, containing 29 acres, one rood and 17 perches, Irish measure, 'with liberty to use the wharf or quay facing the premises', to Paul Hale and his brothers, William and John, 'for their natural life or survivor of them' for a term of 99 years at the yearly rent of £25-15-0.[1] Margaret Holmes, a widow from Harold's Cross, Dublin, and the only child of Paul Hale, later inherited the lease. In 1796, she assigned the land to her son John Holmes, to pay off her debts and to give her an annuity of £100 a year for her life.[2] Over the following years, the land was sub-leased to various tenants. In August 1814, a newspaper advertisement stated that Sergeant John Ball, deceased, had recently built the Thornhill house, and the 'mansion house, offices, garden and demesne, situated one mile beyond Clontarf' were now for sale or to let immediately. The estate contained 56 Irish acres 'held by leases for terms of years, of which 28 are unexpired and subject to the yearly rent of £206-2-4.'[3] As Sergeant Ball had leased 28 Irish acres of land in the adjoining parish of Raheny in 1813, paying a yearly rent of

£115-10-0,[4] this land was obviously included in the total acreage for his Thornhill estate when it was advertised in 1814. Despite all the sub-leasing of the Thornhill estate over the years, the Holmes family managed to hold on to the original lease of 1747. In 1829, this lease was put in trust to William Jameson and William Mulock, to provide an income for James Paul Holmes, the son of John Holmes and Margaret Holmes's grandson, on his intended marriage to Catherine Mulock.[5]

In April 1835, Arthur Lee and Benjamin Lee paid £500 to Hugh O'Reilly, who had now acquired an interest in the lease and whose family was living at Thornhill since 1829. O'Reilly held a lease in two plots of land at Blackbush, Clontarf. The first plot related to the original land leased by John Vernon to Paul Hale, where the Thornhill house was situated, with an entrance from the coast road. The second plot of land was for two acres, two roods and 16 perches, Irish measure, called the Upper Meadow, which adjoined Thornhill, and had been added to the estate by 1809. A second entrance to Thornhill from Blackbush Lane (now known as Mount Prospect Avenue) cut through this Upper Meadow.[6] The following month, May 1835, Arthur Lee and Benjamin Lee paid £1,600 to William Jameson and William Henry Mulock, the trustees of the original lease of John Vernon to Paul Hale.[7]

The Guinness brothers obviously moved into their new home at once because their address was given as Thornhill when they signed two new leases for the land with John Edward Venables Vernon of Clontarf Castle two months later on 21 July 1835. The first lease was for the Thornhill house and land at Blackbush, Clontarf, to hold from 15 March 1835 for the term of 200 years at the yearly rent of £111-10-10.[8] The second lease was for the land called Upper Meadow, Blackbush, to hold from 25 March 1846, when the original lease from Vernon was due to expire, for a term of 189 years at the yearly rent of £12-6-11.[9] The total area of the two properties in English statute was approximately 50 acres. The maps on these original leases, presently held by Dublin City Council, show great detail about the house and land divisions on the Thornhill estate in 1835, and as this was two years before the Ordnance Survey began, add greatly to the knowledge about the original estate.

THE ORIGIN OF ST ANNE'S HOUSE AND ESTATE

Surprisingly, the day after signing the new leases with John E.V. Vernon, the Guinness brothers mortgaged the main property Thornhill and its land back to the trustees, William Jameson and William Henry Mulock, with proviso of redemption on payment of £1,600 with interest.[10] It seems strange that the Guinness brothers should mortgage the main property back to the trustees within a few weeks. Perhaps the trustees wanted to hold on to the original lease until the end of its term, which had another 11 years to run. Perhaps the Guinness brothers did not have the ready cash at that time, owing to other business commitments. The mortgage was registered in the Registry of Deeds, but not the repayment, which was the normal practice at that time. It is only speculation why the property was mortgaged; whatever the reason, the mortgage was repaid after a few years as the Guinness family stayed and made it their home. This was the beginning of the Guinness estate in Clontarf.

Within a few months of moving into Thornhill, the Guinness brothers had also acquired adjoining land in the parish of Raheny from the Ball family. It is probable that the Mrs Ball recorded in the Tithes Applotment Books for Raheny Parish in 1830 as occupier of 22 Irish acres, which equalled 36 English statute acres, was the widow of the previously mentioned Sergeant Ball who built Thornhill. The following year, in June 1836, Ellen Ball, late of Raheny Cottage but now living in Paris, leased 36 acres in Raheny to Arthur Lee and Benjamin Lee Guinness. The lease stated that the Guinness brothers were already in possession of the land and that it was for a term of 14 years from 1 November 1835 at the yearly rent of £91-8-6. This deed is not registered in the Registry of Deeds, but details were given in a later deed in 1838.[11] From checking all the records of Griffith's Valuation, with the corresponding maps of the Valuation Office and the Ordnance Survey, these 36 acres in Raheny are identified as 26 acres in Bettyville townland and 10 acres in Charleville townland, both adjoining the Thornhill property. With the acquisition of this land, the size of the Guinness estate at Clontarf/Raheny was now about 86 acres.

Within a short period of acquiring the property, Benjamin Lee started to make changes and improvements. The fact that he married his first

St Anne's: The Story of a Guinness Estate

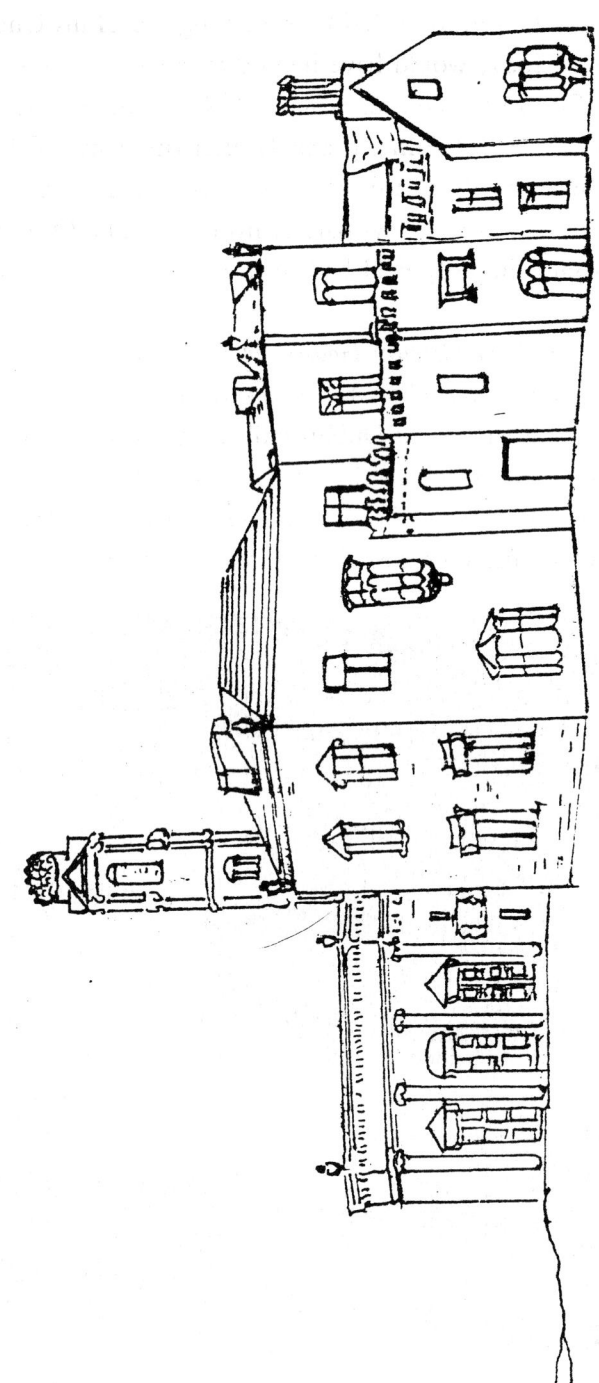

Sketch of St Ann's House c. 1837 with Roman tower on roof. *From the notebook of Henry Hill, Irish Architectural Archives (IAA)*.

cousin Elizabeth Guinness (called Bessie), daughter of his Uncle Edward, on 24 February 1837, would have been a factor in his decision to build a new house for himself and his wife, and also to develop the estate. He called this new house St Ann's, probably after the name of the holy well located on the east side of the Naniken River in Bettyville townland, Raheny Parish, which was now part of his estate. The Ordnance Survey Name books said the holy well had been a place of pilgrimage in years gone by.

In his *Guide to Irish Country Houses,* Mark Bence-Jones states that the original Georgian house Thornhill was pulled down circa 1850 and an Italianate house by Millard of Dublin built in its stead.[12] But this account is not accurate. The shape and size of the Thornhill house is clearly outlined in the map drawn on the original deed of 21 July 1835 from John Vernon to the Guinness brothers. Two years later, in 1837, the manuscript

St Ann's Well after which the estate was named. *Dublin City Council.*

map of the first edition of the Ordnance Survey, called the 'Fair Plan', was drawn, and it showed a difference in the size, the shape and also the name of the house. It seems, therefore, that the new house, St Ann's, was built either late in 1836 or early in 1837, and incorporated part of the original house, Thornhill. These points are also verified by looking at a copy of a sketch of the house, taken circa 1837 by the architect, Henry Hill, and now held by the Irish Architectural Archives. This sketch shows St Ann's as an odd-shaped Italian style house, with an unusual observation tower on the roof.[13] The tower measured 11 feet in length, 11 feet in breath and 36 feet in height (3.35 × 3.35 × 11 metres).[14] It was a replica of the Roman Tomb of the Julii at St Rémy in France, and was removed many years later by Benjamin Lee's son, Arthur Edward, and resited on a mound overlooking the lake where it still stands today.[15] From studying the surveyed plans of the house drawn up by Dublin Corporation in 1941, it seems that a wing of the original Thornhill house was kept in both Benjamin Lee's house and also the later house remodelled by his son, Arthur Edward, when the builder was Thomas Millard.[16]

The Ordnance Survey Fair Plan map of 1837 clearly shows St Ann's house with the same two entrances as when the house was called Thornhill, one from the strand road and the other at the top of Blackbush Lane. The Ordnance Survey Name Books for Co. Dublin describe St Ann's as 'a modern two storey house in good repair, with office houses slated and well laid-out gardens on the north side of the house'. The name of the house and holy well is shown and spelt on the maps as St Ann's, but over the years the extra 'e' has been added to the spelling, and the estate and house have become generally known as St Anne's.

Frederick Darley Ogilby records in his diary a description of St Anne's house and estate at this period. His mother was Elizabeth Darley, daughter of Alderman Frederick Darley and his wife, Elizabeth Guinness, who was a first cousin of Benjamin Lee. Frederick had been reared in America and later became a distinguished clergyman. In April 1840 he came to visit his Irish cousins and was charmed by the wealth and sophisticated lifestyle of all his Guinness relatives. He wrote that St Anne's 'is situated on Dublin Bay most beautifully. The house has a castle-like appearance

THE ORIGIN OF ST ANNE'S HOUSE AND ESTATE

being of irregular Gothic construction with a high tower rising from the centre. The prospect from this is very extensive and commanding.' He found the interior of the house magnificent, and was astonished that the fretwork ceiling in one of the rooms alone cost £1,500. 'There is a splendid organ and the greatest profusion of the costliest furniture.'[17] Benjamin Lee obviously spent money on making an impressive and luxurious new home for his wife and family.

Roman tower removed from the roof of the original house and resited overlooking the lake. *J. Sharkey*

In January 1838, Arthur Lee sold his half share in St Anne's to his brother Benjamin Lee for £1,846.[18] The reason behind this move was twofold. First, Benjamin Lee was now married and St Anne's had become the family home, whereas Arthur Lee remained a bachelor. The second and more pressing reason was that Arthur Lee was in financial difficulties and sought help from his father Arthur and his brother Benjamin Lee. This crisis was overcome when they paid off his debts. Shortly afterwards, Arthur Lee, at his own request, also withdrew from the brewery partnership and, with a £12,000 settlement, went to live in Stillorgan Park, Co. Dublin.

Arthur Lee did not have the temperament for business. He seems to have been the complete opposite in character to the rest of the family, and his days at Stillorgan were spent composing verse in praise of nature and collecting pictures. He died there in 1863.[19] His generosity as a compassionate landlord during the great Famine was recorded by his tenants, who presented him with a miniature commemorative obelisk of green Connemara marble, based on an original that stood on his estate. The second Lord Allen erected the obelisk, designed by Sir Edward Levett Pearce, in the grounds of Stillorgan Park in 1727. This obelisk stands over 100 feet high, and today is clearly visible beside modern housing on Carysfort Avenue, Blackrock, Co. Dublin. The miniature obelisk, only 18 inches (45.7 centimetres) high, was kept for many years in the directors' offices at Guinness's brewery in Dublin, and bears the following inscription:

1847

To Arthur Lee Guinness Esq

Stilorgan Park

To mark the veneration of his faithfull labourers who in a period of dire distress were protected by his generous liberality from the prevailing destitution.

This humble testimonial is respectfully dedicated consisting of home material.

Its colour serves to remind that the memory of benefits will ever remain green in Irish hearts.[20]

CHAPTER FOUR

Development of the Estate and Gardens

Benjamin Lee Guinness at this time was the controlling partner in the brewery and was living with his growing family in St Anne's. In 1839, he built an ornamental tower bridge over the entrance drive from the coast road at his estate to mark the occasion of the birth of his first child, Anne Lee. After the birth of Anne, Benjamin and his wife Bessie then had three sons: Arthur Edward, born in 1840; Benjamin Lee, in 1842; and Edward Cecil, in 1847.

In keeping with his position and wealth, Benjamin Lee began to enlarge the estate of St Anne's whenever an opportunity arose to acquire land. By January 1838, when he bought out his brother's half share in the St Anne's estate, the total area of the estate was 86 acres, made up of the original 50 acres in Clontarf parish, plus the 36 acres in Raheny parish. By 1848, Griffith's Primary Valuation shows that the amount of land occupied by Benjamin Lee in Raheny was now 45 acres, an increase of nine acres, which was mainly reclaimed pasture land at the sea shore in Bettyville townland.[1] The estate now contained 95 acres. The Valuation also records that Benjamin Lee had a new next-door neighbour in Bettyville townland, a Patrick Boland, who now occupied Watermill House with 13 acres. *Thom's Directory* records Patrick Boland as a baker in Capel Street, Dublin with a residence at Watermill, Raheny.

By 1850, the lease of the original 36 acres in Raheny which Benjamin Lee had secured from Ellen Ball had expired. When Benjamin Lee went to the Earl of Howth to get a new lease for the Raheny land, he ended up losing several acres in the Bettyville townland to his neighbour, Patrick Boland. Why this happened is not clear. As the Earl of Howth was the owner of the land, he was free to lease it to whoever he pleased.

Possibly Patrick Boland was anxious to get more land in the area to grow wheat for his bakery business and approached the Earl of Howth for additional land in Bettyville. Whatever the reason, it appears that Patrick Boland got a long lease of this land; the actual date of the acquisition is not known, as it was not registered but was mentioned in another lease in 1874, over 20 years later, as being a lease of 150 years.[2] Besides getting the extra land in Bettyville townland, the Valuation Books in 1855 record that Patrick Boland had also become occupier of 49 acres in the nearby townland of Raheny South, which he was subleasing from Joseph Kincaid, a land agent with an address at Leinster Street, Dublin.

Benjamin Lee signed a new lease with the Earl of Howth for 22 acres only in Raheny, on 29 April 1850. The lease was for a term of 99 years from 1 November 1849 at the yearly rent of £76-14-6, and interestingly

Tower bridge built over the entrance drive from the coast road to commemorate the birth of Anne Lee Guinness in 1839. *Plunket collection.*

it was witnessed by the above-mentioned land agent, Joseph Kincaid.[3] The Valuation Books in 1855 record this land as 23 acres, made up of 10 acres in Charleville and 13 acres in Bettyville, and the land previously occupied by Benjamin Lee in Bettyville is shown as now occupied by Patrick Boland. The Gaisford-St Lawrence family in Howth Castle presently hold a survey of the Howth estate taken in 1863. This survey confirms that Benjamin Lee Guinness occupied the above 23 acres in Bettyville and Charleville townlands and that Patrick Boland was occupier of 38 acres in Bettyville, surrounding Watermill House, as well as the 49 acres in Raheny South, previously mentioned, sublet from Joseph Kincaid.[4] The total acreage of St Anne's was now reduced to 73 acres.

Although Benjamin Lee had now lost land on the eastern side of St Anne's estate in Raheny parish, within a few years he had acquired more land on the western side in Clontarf parish. Bedford Lodge, an eighteenth-century house and demesne, lay adjacent to St Anne's at Blackbush Lane. Benjamin Lee acquired the house and 12 acres of land on lease from John E.V. Vernon for 61 years from 25 March 1854 at the yearly rent of £80.[5]

This acquisition combined two holdings, one of nine acres at Bedford Lodge, plus three acres of the old village of Blackbush or Heronstown which formerly had been situated at the corner of Blackbush Lane and the strand road.[6] In 1837 the Ordnance Survey map clearly shows this village, and the Ordnance Survey Name Books describes it as a small village of about 15 mud houses, while the Valuation Field Books and House Books of 1845 list 21 houses. Three years later, according to Griffith's Valuation, all the houses except one have been removed and the land is shown as building ground in fee to John E.V. Vernon. The removal of the houses is also confirmed by looking at the census returns. In 1841, there were a total of 31 houses in the Heronstown townland, which by 1851 had fallen to 16, a reduction of 15 houses, while the population fell accordingly from 174 people in 1841 to 106 by 1851.[7] The living conditions of the people who lived in these mud houses in the Blackbush/Heronstown village were most likely very primitive and Vernon wanted to pull the houses down. Ten years previously, he was very anxious to get rid of the unsightly and unsanitary houses belonging to about 200 families of the fisherman at 'The Sheds' in Clontarf. When granting a lease for Reverend James Callanan, PP of Clontarf to build a new church for the site in 1835, Vernon gave the lease on condition that the PP would do away with 'The Sheds'. Some of these families were rehoused in new cottages nearby while others were given compensation.[8] But the fate of the Blackbush villagers is not known. The little village of mud houses was gone and the land became part of St Anne's estate.

James Colvill, a Governor of the Bank of Ireland, occupied Bedford Lodge in 1845, and a James Nixon was recorded as occupier in 1848. When Benjamin Lee acquired the lease in 1854, he let the house firstly to John J. Walker, a teacher in Clontarf. By 1865 the Misses Mary and Sarah Stapleton had became the occupiers, and these two sisters lived in the house for the next 40 years.[9] By 1855, the total area of St Anne's, following these transactions, was around 85 acres, i.e. 62 acres in Clontarf

Map showing St Ann's estate, Bedford Lodge and Blackbush village. *OS Map, 6 inch, sheet 19, surveyed 1837, corrected to 1843.*

parish and 23 acres in Raheny parish. This was the extent of St Anne's estate for the rest of Benjamin Lee's life, as no further acquisitions took place.

The beautiful landscaped gardens at St Anne's must have taken Benjamin Lee many years to create. The panoramic view of Dublin Bay from the estate, with the cones of the Great and Little Sugar Loaf Mountains silhouetted against the sky, reminded him of the Bay of Naples in Italy, and this influenced his layout of the gardens and also possibly the house. A water-temple, based on a Pompeian model, was erected on the artifical lake formed by damming the Naniken river, and a Herculanean temple was also built overlooking the river. The central walk of the formal walled garden behind the house was made into 'an outdoor sculpture gallery for a collection of marble statuary' bought by Benjamin Lee on his travels in Italy, with a background of castellated yew hedges. Another garden had a circular yew hedge with alcoves and arches in which stood 'allegorical Italian statues', all reflected in a great circular fountain in the centre.[10] The walled vegetable garden was entered through gates under a four-storey brick clock tower, which had a giant bell, dated 1850 and inscribed with Benjamin Lee's name and family motto, *Spes Mea in Deo* (My Hope is in God).[11] Later a large conservatory was added to the east side of the house.

Benjamin Lee was deeply religious and took an active part in the local parish life of the Church of Ireland in Raheny. Only a few years after moving into his new home at St Anne's, he had made a proposal at the Easter Vestry meeting in April 1839 to build a new church on a different site in Raheny. Nothing further became of this resolution, as obviously no suitable land became available in the village for the building of this new church.[12] He also became a trustee of the Raheny Infant School, on Station Road, which he served until his death.

The formal garden with castellated yew hedge and classical Italian statues. *Gillman collection*.

The Clock Tower, covered in ivy, built as the entrance to the walled-in garden. *Plunket collection*.

Pompeian Temple beside the lake. *Gillman collection, IAA.*

Herculanean Temple overlooking the Naniken river. *J. Sharkey.*

CHAPTER FIVE

The Ascending Years

The second Arthur Guinness lived a long life and died in June 1855 at the age of 87. He had set up many large family trust funds during his life and still managed to leave a personal estate of £150,000,[1] including £600 towards the benefit of his local church and school in Coolock, Co. Dublin.

Benjamin Lee was 57 when his father died. He had worked for nearly 40 years in the brewery and as a partner for 35 of these years. Although he had almost total control during the later years of his father's life, assisted by the able partnership of John Purser Jnr, he always listened to and sought his father's advice on many matters. After John Purser Jnr's death in 1858, Benjamin Lee was in sole control of the brewery. He seemed content to wait until after his father's death to take a prominent role in business and public life. In the 13 years after the death of Arthur, he seemed to be a man in a hurry to make up for lost time. This period manifested Benjamin Lee's great industrial achievements and he became the most prominent and successful figure in Irish business life. He also laid the foundation of a family dynasty, which later reached the highest echelons of both Irish and British society.

During Benjamin Lee's later years, production at James's Gate advanced rapidly and the brewery was often enlarged and remodelled to keep pace with sales. In Dublin there were ten other firms making brown stout, but the Guinness output was as great as their combined production. Only four other breweries in the United Kingdom exceeded Guinness's production. A decision by Benjamin Lee in April 1862 really stamped the 'Irishness' of Guinness stout on the world market and was a major marketing initiative. He decided to use the Brian Boru harp, which is today preserved in Trinity College, Dublin, as the Guinness trade mark, and the first labels were issued on 18 August 1862.[2] Perhaps the idea for this famous trade mark was inspired by the fact that his St Anne's estate was situated in Clontarf, where Brian Boru, High King of Ireland, defeated the Norsemen in the historic battle in 1014.

Benjamin Lee continued to divide his time between the brewery town house in Thomas Street and his St Anne's estate with his family. As apparently no further opportunity for acquiring land at St Anne's occurred, he turned his attention and his growing wealth to acquiring other properties elsewhere.

In the aftermath of the Famine, many estates throughout Ireland were bankrupt and the opportunities arose for those with money to buy properties, often at a reasonable price. The Encumbered Estates Court was established by an Act of 1849 to facilitate the transfer of debt-ridden estates from bankruptcy to solvent owners. The Landed Estates Court, established by the Act, had the power to pay creditors out of the purchase price and to guarantee title to the new owner.

Over a ten-year period, the courts disposed of over 3,000 estates. It was under this court that Benjamin Lee acquired his substantial tracts of land in Co. Mayo and Co. Galway. Apparently he first became attracted to the area when visiting the ancient Abbey at Cong, and when the nearby Ashford estate was put up for sale in 1852, Benjamin Lee bought it in fee simple. He paid £11,005 for the Ashford demesne and its 480 acres plus another 698 acres nearby.[3] Ashford was a former shooting lodge situated on a beautiful position on the shore of Lough Corrib and was owned by Lord Oranmore and Browne, whose family had lived there for centuries. Over the next couple of years, Benjamin Lee spent a considerable amount of money buying several other estates nearby, and thus became the largest owner of land, holding about 14,400 acres that stretched from the shores of Lough Corrib to those of Lough Mask.

This area of Connemara had suffered greatly during and after the Famine, and when Benjamin Lee acquired the estate, he created much employment and greatly improved the living standards of the local people. He made additions to the house and undertook many improvements on the estate, including major road building, land reclamation and drainage.[4] Benjamin Lee also undertook restoration of the ancient Abbey of Cong. His interest and support for the Church of Ireland in the locality was significant. He paid for the stained glass windows in St Mary's Church, which was built in 1855 in the village of Cong. He also provided the money for a new tower and spire to be added to the church, which was built by Timothy Murphy and Sons, Amiens Street, Dublin, and cost £670. An inscription on the tower states it was completed in 1861. He later donated a site to the Bishop of Tuam in 1864 to build a church at Castlekirke, which was situated a few miles west of Cong, on the shore of Lough Corrib.[5]

In 1856, the year following his father's death, Benjamin Lee decided to acquire a substantial town house, in keeping with his increased wealth and status as the leading merchant in Dublin City. Number 80 St Stephen's Green was an eighteenth-century town mansion, built by

80/81 St Stephen's Green bought in 1856 and remodelled to the above design by Benjamin Lee Guinness as his town house. Donated by his grandson to the nation in 1939 and renamed Iveagh House. *Department of Foreign Affairs.*

Bishop Clayton to Richard Castle's designs in one of Dublin's fashionable squares. Benjamin Lee bought it from the Encumbered Estates for £2,500.[6] He later acquired the adjoining property and converted the two into one house with a unified facade of Portland stone and also acted as architect himself for the remodelling. From then on it became the Guinness family's town house, establishing a tradition of splendid entertaining for three generations of brewers.[7] The old town house in Thomas Street was then converted into offices.

Benjamin Lee had been elected Lord Mayor of Dublin in 1851, and after that he was pressed many times to stand for Parliament. But his father's advice to him was that politics would not be good for brewery business and he refused all offers during the lifetime of his father. But ten years later, in 1865, he felt these considerations were no longer valid as the brewery was thriving, and he decided to stand for election and was duly elected Conservative and Unionist Member for Dublin City.[8]

Although Benjamin Lee and his family were surrounded by opulence, 'their lives were sober – in some ways austere – and the day began and ended with family prayers'.[9] Benjamin Lee, like his father, was deeply religious; he respected his wealth and felt it was a sacred trust to be used for the good of others. Over the years, the family was regarded as a benevolent employer, and workers at the brewery had job security with many health and social benefits.

Benjamin Lee also used his wealth for the benefit of his native city. Among his many public enterprises was his involvement, along with other prominent citizens, in the Dublin Exhibition of Arts and Industries, which was opened by the Prince of Wales in May 1865. But his greatest contribution to the city of Dublin was his generosity in restoring St Patrick's Cathedral from falling into ruin after years of decay and neglect. Neither the church nor the state had the money or the inclination to undertake the project. The restoration took several years and aroused a lot of interest. There were frequent comments in Ireland's leading architectural journal, the *Dublin Builder*, about progress on the restoration. He personally spent between £110,000 and £150,000 on the total cost of the restoration.[10]

His many acts of generosity did not go unrecognised by the establishment and in 1867 Benjamin Lee was created a Baronet.[11] This was the first title to be bestowed on a member of the Guinness family. He did not live long to enjoy it, as he died suddenly in London on 19 May 1868 in his seventieth year. His body was brought back to Dublin and his funeral from St Anne's Clontarf to interment at Mount Jerome Cemetery was an impressive demonstration of public sorrow, with over 500 carriages and a thousand working men, walking four deep, covering a length of two miles through the city.[12] A few years after his death, in recognition of his generous support to St Patrick's Cathedral, a statue by the sculptor John Henry Foley was erected in the grounds of the cathedral.[13]

At the time of his death, James's Gate was the largest porter brewery in the world.[14] The extent of the success that he achieved could be seen when his will was probated. Although he had spent money on many projects over the years and had set up various family trusts before his death, Sir Benjamin Lee was still able to leave an estate valued at over one million pounds, making it the largest will proved in Ireland up to that date.[15] He was Ireland's first millionaire. Benjamin Lee married late and did not live long enough to see his sons marry, but in his lifetime he witnessed the meteoric rise of his family from respected merchants towards the higher realms of civic honours, politics and social prominence. He had the pleasure of seeing his only daughter, Anne Lee, bring a title into the family by her marriage in 1863 to the Church of Ireland clergyman William Cunningham Plunket, later to become Archbishop of Dublin and the fourth Baron Plunket. As his second son, Benjamin Lee, had embarked on a military career, the main part of Sir Benjamin Lee's estate was left equally between his eldest son, Arthur Edward, and his youngest son, Edward Cecil, with both as co-partners in the brewery. The brothers were very young men to be left in control of such a substantial business: Arthur was 27 years old and Edward was only 20. Arthur had been educated at Eton in England and Trinity College, Dublin, while his younger brother Edward started working in the brewery at 15, and had commenced studying part time at Trinity when his father died.

The extent and changes to the estates at the time of Sir Benjamin Lee's death in 1868 outlined above. *OS Map, 6 inch, sheet 19, revised 1869.*

Sir Benjamin Lee was a far-seeing industrialist and wanted the capital of the brewery to be kept intact and not squandered among his heirs to use outside the business. He had seen too many members of his own extended family unable to use their wealth wisely over the years, and was determined that the brewery would not be milked for their benefit. The deed of partnership stipulated in his will that if either of his sons decided to leave the business, the retiring son would be obliged to turn over his half share to the other son, and would only get the small sum of £30,000 upon retirement, paid over eight years. This sum represented only a pittance in comparison to the million-pound value of his estate. Perhaps Sir Benjamin Lee had a shrew idea as to which of his sons was best suited to become the brewer of the family. He left the town mansion in Stephen's Green, not far from the brewery, to the younger son, Edward Cecil, while the country estates of St Anne's and Ashford were left to his eldest son, Arthur Edward.[16] His legacy to his native city and country was immense, and he lay the foundation from which his descendants rose to the heights of the British Establishment.

CHAPTER SIX

Major Expansions

St Anne's estate as we know it today owes its expansion and development mainly to Sir Arthur Edward Guinness and his wife Olive. Arthur was born on 1 November 1840 at St Anne's. After leaving Eton, he obtained an MA degree from Trinity College, Dublin in 1866. As the eldest son he inherited his father's baronetcy and his parliamentary seat upon his death in 1868. In the general election later that year, he was again returned, but the following year he was unseated on a petition, as it was found that his agents had been guilty of taking bribes, although he himself was not involved.[1] This kept him out of parliament for the next five years. On 16 February 1871 in the parish church of Bantry, West Cork, he married Lady Olive Charlotte White, the daughter of William, third Earl of Bantry. Sir Arthur was then aged 30, while Lady Olive was only 20.[2] Now that he had married into the nobility, it seemed Sir Arthur turned his energy and his money into acquiring first a town house at 18 Lower Leeson Street, in Dublin, and then expanding his estate at St Anne's whenever land became available. He also took an active part in affairs relating to the Clontarf and Raheny areas. Sir Arthur was one of the original commissioners of the Clontarf Township when it was set up in 1869 under the chairmanship of John E.V. Vernon, of Clontarf Castle, and he continued to serve as a commissioner until Clontarf was absorbed into the city in 1900.[3]

His commitment to Raheny Parish was very prominent, as he took a special interest in all activities relating to the Established Church and schools. From early in the sixteenth century until 1869, the Church of Ireland or Anglican Church was the State or Established Church in Ireland. Gladstone's Act of Disestablishment of the Church of Ireland came into force on 1 January 1871. As a result, many parishes like Raheny faced financial difficulties, as the glebe land and income were confiscated, yet the parish had only a small community to maintain a church, a rector and a school. Into the breach stepped Sir Arthur Guinness. Both St Assam's Church and the Parochial School beside it were now vested in the Representative Body of the Church of Ireland. In a letter to a special meeting of the Select Vestry of Raheny parish, in December 1872, Sir Arthur proposed to contribute to the endowment of the parish. In return, he wanted the future right of presentation of a rector to himself and his heirs. This was an unusual proposal, but the parish gratefully accepted it. In January 1873, Sir Arthur was registered as a vestry member and shortly afterwards he nominated the Reverend Francis Hayes as rector of Raheny parish, where he served for over 40 years.[4]

John Maunsell, a solicitor, was church warden in Raheny and lived in the nearby Edenmore House, formerly called Violet Hill. In 1874 John Maunsell and Sir Arthur Guinness acquired the rectory house and five acres of glebe land for the benefit of the parish.[5] Now the future of both the church and the rectory were secured. At this time also, Sir Arthur and John Maunsell were anxious about the future ownership of the Raheny Parochial School, which was situated beside the church and graveyard. Samuel Dick of Violet Hill had built both the Parochial School and the eight Crescent Cottages in the village in the late eighteenth century. In his will in 1802, he bequeathed the income from the rents of the cottages for the salary of the schoolmaster. By 1879, the school was very badly attended, and the teacher, Alexander Lyon, had built an extension at one end from where he ran the village post office, while renting out another room as the dispensary. To secure the ownership of the building, Sir Arthur obtained the title from the Representative Body of the Church of Ireland by buying off Alexander Lyon, who lived there until his death in 1889. Sir Arthur had the school building renovated and it was later used as a post office, a dispensary, and a residence. As the Crescent cottages at this time were also in need of repair, Sir Arthur spent £375 on their renovations.[6]

Sir Arthur also became involved with the Raheny Infant School, situated opposite the railway station, and he took his father's place as a trustee of this school in 1868. By 1875 this school was in poor condition and a

MAJOR EXPANSIONS

Sir Arthur Edward Guinness, Lord Ardilaun (1840–1915). *Courtesy of the National Library of Ireland, R 27817.*

new red-brick school, including accommodation for the teacher, was built on the same site, with again both Sir Arthur and John Maunsell contributing two thirds of the cost. Most children had now transferred from the old Parochial School beside the graveyard and this new Infant School had become the main Raheny Parish School. It became a national school in 1886, and today is used as a Montessori school.[7]

At St Anne's Sir Arthur turned his energy and money in undertaking major expansion. This occurred in two phases. The first involved the acquisition of lands over a relatively short four-year period, from 1874 up to 1878. The second phase involved an extensive building programme on the house, and the landscaping of the grounds, as well as commissioning new buildings within the estate.

CHAPTER SEVEN

Acquisitions: 1874–1875

The first step by Sir Arthur to enlarge the estate at St Anne's was taken in February 1874, when he negotiated a new lease for Bedford Lodge with John E.V. Vernon of Clontarf Castle. This involved surrendering the original lease of 26 May 1854 signed by his father, Sir Benjamin Lee, but included the acquisition of two other portions of land nearby. One was for two fields of seven acres in Heronstown townland, situated on the corner of Blackbush Lane and the coast road, opposite the land of Bedford Lodge. The second lot consisted of three fields with a cottage of 20 acres in Greenlanes townland, further up Blackbush Lane, which was situated next to the land of Seapark House, and opposite Mount Prospect House. The new lease was for a term of 200 years from 25 March 1873 at the yearly rent of £405, with the intention of erecting substantial buildings within two years on the land of Bedford Lodge.[1] It was a few years before Sir Arthur got round to building on this land. Bedford Lodge house continued to be let to Mary Stapleton. With this lease, the St Anne's estate increased from 85 acres to 112 acres.

The biggest acquisition of land took place just a few months later, in June 1874, when Sir Arthur with one lease secured almost one third of the land of Raheny parish from William Ulick Tristram, the fourth Earl of Howth. William had succeeded his father Thomas, the third Earl, who had died a few months previously, in February 1874. Sir Arthur paid a high price for the lease, which involved an initial sum of £12,000, plus two further sums of £3,000, making a total of £18,000. The lease was for a term of 500 years from 1 November 1873, paying the yearly rent of £814-2-2. The total area was 277 acres and covered the greater part of the townlands of Raheny South, Bettyville, Charleville and Maryville.

Although this lease involved a large area of the parish of Raheny, in fact only a small number of people were actually living on this land. The lease was subject to the leases and tenancies in the following schedule:[2]

Tenants' Name	Statute Measure (Acre–Rood–Perch)	Rent (£–s–d)	Tenure
1. Patrick Fottrell	36–0–27	102–15–0	Year to Year
2. Joseph Kincaid	78–3–1	170–12–8	Lease for life of lessee
3. John Harden	17–2–18	95–0–0	Year to Year
4. John Harden	29–2–25	62–0–0	Year to Year
5. Sir A.E. Guinness	23–1–29	76–14–6	Lease expires 1948
6. Patrick Boland	39–2–29	200–0–0	Lease for 150 years
7. Anthony Toole	52–0–3	130–0–0	Lease expires 1878
Total:	277–1–12	837–2–2	
Less Annual Cess		23–0–0	
Total		814–2–2	

One could well ask how Sir Arthur managed to obtain such a large amount of land all together in one swoop, and also take over as occupier within a few years. This was due to a number of circumstances.

The most important fact was that William, the fourth Earl of Howth, was short of money and had heavy mortgages to pay, whereas Sir Arthur was wealthy, and able to pay a high price to acquire more land in the area to enlarge his estate. The third Earl of Howth had mortgaged most of his land in Dublin and Meath, which included all the parish of Raheny, to the Bank of Ireland for £65,000, and in 1871 the bank was looking for repayment. The Representative Church Body paid off this debt to the bank and took over the mortgage.[3] Selling a lease of land in Raheny for a total of £18,000 must have greatly eased the Earl of Howth's financial problems.

But it is more than likely that the initial impetus for Sir Arthur to acquire the land, was due to the vacancy at Watermill House and lands which adjoined St Anne's estate. Patrick Boland had been in occupation of the property in Bettyville townland since 1848 and was the only one of the above tenants, besides Sir Arthur himself, who held a long lease. Although Patrick Boland is listed in the above deed and schedule, in fact he was not alive when the lease was signed, having died at Watermill House three years earlier on 12 December 1871.[4] After his death, his wife Elizabeth signed a new lease for the Watermill lands with the Earl of Howth on 19 July 1872,[5] but she also died a few months later, on 29 November 1872.[6] Watermill House is shown as vacant in *Thom's Directory* for 1873 and 1874. It seems likely that the deaths of the Bolands may have been the opportunity for Sir Arthur to obtain extra land in Raheny. He may have approached the Earl of Howth to obtain this land, seeing as some of it had once formed part of the original St Anne's estate, which his father Sir Benjamin Lee lost in 1850. There was also the possibility that Sir Arthur was interested in renegotiating a longer lease for his Bettyville land while also acquiring more land in the area at this time, and the resulting land transaction was beneficial to both the Earl of Howth and Sir Arthur.

The other people listed in the above deed had only yearly leases, and within a few years, Sir Arthur was in occupation of all these lands. Both Patrick Fottrell, who had a holding in Maryville, and John Harden, whose holdings were in Maryville and Charleville, only had leases from year to year, so Sir Arthur obviously did not renew them. According to the Valuation Books, Patrick Fottrell had become occupier of his land in Maryville by 1862, and as there was no house on this land, he must have only farmed there and lived elsewhere. He is not listed in any Dublin directories but he could have been related to other Fottrells listed in nearby parishes: Joseph, a contractor in Kilbarrack; Walter, a farmer and vintner in Belcamp, Coolock; and William, a farmer in St Doulough's, Balgriffin.

John Harden is listed in many directories as Superintendent of City of Dublin Steam Packet Company, with residences at Number 45 Buckingham Street, Dublin and Brighton Lodge, Maryville, Raheny; but by 1876 he is listed only at his town address and has left Brighton Lodge. Thirty years previously, the description of Brighton Lodge in the Valuation House Book is of 'an old farm house, built of bad material and added to by each succeeding tenant, and fast going to decay'. The Valuation Books show that Sir Arthur had demolished the house by 1879.[7]

ACQUISITIONS: 1874–1875

Joseph Kincaid had acquired his lease in the Raheny South townland in 1841.[8] As described previously, he was listed in many Dublin directories over the years as a land agent in Leinster Street, Dublin, with residences at Herbert Street and Monkstown, and was a witness to the 1850 lease for the 22 acres in Raheny to Sir Benjamin Lee. That land was inherited by Sir Arthur, whose lease was due to expire in 1948, as shown in the above schedule. Kincaid had sublet his land in Raheny South to three local people, two of whom already occupied other land nearby. He sublet 49 acres to Patrick Boland of Watermill House, which was now unoccupied. Another 20 acres were let to Anthony O'Toole, who also had a lease in Bettyville and Charleville from Lord Howth. The remaining six acres were let to Felix McGowran.[9] A year later in December 1875 Joseph Kincaid died,[10] and as the lease was only for his lifetime, Sir Arthur was therefore able to take over his holdings. By 1876, Sir Arthur is recorded as occupier of all this land in the Valuation Cancelled Books.

Felix McGowran was listed in many Dublin directories as a jaunting car, cart and car maker whose premises were situated in Ballyhoy townland across the Howth Road from where he rented the six acres from Kincaid in Raheny South townland. He leased the principal public house in the village in 1843, which today is called The Station House. Later he acquired land in the Snug townland of Raheny and in Heronstown, Clontarf, opposite St Anne's estate.[11] Over the years he became a very successful businessman in Raheny village. Losing his six acres in Raheny may not have bothered him too much, as he had acquired more land nearby.

The Schedule above shows that Anthony O'Toole held 52 acres on lease, which was due to expire in four years time, in 1878. As his lease was not registered in the Registry of Deeds, we have no details of the terms; but from examining the Valuation Books, we can identify the land, which comprised two holdings. By 1855, O'Toole had taken over a house and 31 acres from Patrick O'Rourke in Bettyville townland, called Millbrook Cottage, as well as 21 acres of land from Sarah Wade in Charleville townland. Both these holdings had been recorded in the Valuation House and Field Books in 1845 as being in lease from Lord Howth at £5 per

St Anne's: The Story of a Guinness Estate

Olive Charlotte White, Lady Ardilaun (1850–1925), in formal dress for the coronation of King Edward VII in 1902. *Courtesy of the National Library of Ireland, R 27818.*

acre. Anthony O'Toole had been listed in *Thom's Directory* for many years as a contractor in Raheny and *Slater's Directory* of 1870 lists him as a farmer and contractor. In January 1874, a few months prior to Sir Arthur acquiring the large tract of the Raheny lands, Anthony O'Toole had acquired a 15-year lease of Darndale House and its 49 acres in the neighbouring parish of Coolock, for which he paid £945.[12]

It is not clear why O'Toole expanded his own land holdings at this time. However, he was obviously very annoyed at losing his land in Raheny when Sir Arthur took over his lease from Lord Howth shortly afterwards. O'Toole was not happy about this leased land being taken from him, and particularly that 'he is not to get any compensation for taking his farm although he has improvements made,'[13] according to the surveyor's notes for October 1876 in the Valuation Cancelled Books. His voice is the only one we know that objected to losing land to Sir Arthur. Afterwards O'Toole was named as occupier of a small house in Raheny village. Unfortunately he didn't live long afterwards, as he died suddenly from a heart attack on 8 February 1880 at Darndale, Coolock, aged 68.[14] He left no will but his son Denis, of Darndale House, took out Letters of Administration which showed that he was a successful farmer and railway contractor, as his estate was valued at under £6,000. By 1880 the Valuation Books show that Sir Arthur had become occupier of O'Toole's land in Raheny, and that Anthony O'Toole and later his son Denis occupied Darndale House in Coolock.

As shown in the schedule above, when Sir Arthur acquired the 277 acres of Raheny land, only a small number of people were actually occupying the land, and all the land was used for agriculture. The Howth Survey of 1863 showed the land was used mostly for growing wheat and oats. The houses he acquired along with the land were Brighton Lodge, Watermill House, Millbrook Cottage, four cottages on the coast road in Bettyville, and two houses in Raheny South townland. All the houses were later used to house workers on the now expanded St Anne's estate. Brighton Lodge, we have noted, was demolished by 1879. Millbrook Cottage was later renamed Bettyville House and the 1901 census records it as a first-class house, with eight windows in front and ten rooms occupied by Andrew Campbell and his family, who was the head gardener at St Anne's for many years. The four cottages on the coast road were recorded as being occupied by lodgers prior to being acquired by Sir Arthur, and these cottages were later used also for the workers on the estate. The two houses in Raheny South townland were situated on Watermill Road, near Main Street in Raheny Village. One house had been used as a dispensary for some years, and later Anthony O'Toole was occupier for a short time. Sir Arthur had these two cottages later replaced by a red-brick detached cottage, used as the post office, and two semi-detached cottages used by workers on the estate.

An interesting postscript occurred in relation to the Watermill lands. As discussed above, Watermill House and lands had been occupied by Patrick and Elizabeth Boland from 1848 until their deaths in 1872. Their son, Patrick Boland Jnr, had taken over the bakery business at 135–136 Capel Street in 1866, and over the next couple of years turned it into the largest bakery in Ireland. He expanded the business by acquiring Pim's Mills on Grand Canal Street, Dublin, which he renamed Boland's Mills. Within a short period Patrick Jnr had become a wealthy man, and had a residence at Belvidere Terrace, Sandymount.[15]

After Sir Arthur acquired the Watermill lands, Boland came back to live in the Raheny area. In October 1875, he took a 99-year lease on the house, Raheny Park, along with 53 acres, from the Earl of Howth.[16] The main entrance to Raheny Park was situated on the coast road, directly opposite Watermill House, where his parents had lived for many years and where, most likely, he had been reared. Sadly, within two years he died at Raheny Park after a short illness, on 17 May 1877, at the young age of 36, leaving his wife Mary with seven young children. Mary only lived for another year in Raheny Park and then went to live at Winton House, Leeson Street, in Dublin. As three members of the Boland family had died within six years of each other, this would have caused some delays in sorting out probate of all their personal and business affairs. The year following her husband's death, Mary must have made a claim for compensation of the original Boland lease on the Watermill land from Sir Arthur Guinness. This accounts for the payment by him of £300 to

Mary Boland on 9 October 1878. This payment was for the surrender of the original lease of 19 July 1872, from the Earl of Howth to Elizabeth Boland, to be merged and extinquished into Sir Arthur Guinness's new lease of the 277 acres of Raheny land.[17]

With this one lease, Sir Arthur had increased his estate at St Anne's to approximately 366 acres. The boundary of the estate started at the entrance to Sybil Hill, ran along the Howth Road as far as Raheny Village, then turned down Watermill Road, continued along the coast road, and up Mount Prospect Avenue. The distance covered was three miles. The following year, on 4 December 1875, Sir Arthur paid £600 to the Commissioners of Church Temporalities in Ireland for the fee simple of six acres of Glebe land, which was situated on the south side of the Howth Road and adjacent to his newly extended estate.[18] St Anne's now covered 372 acres.

During all these land transactions at St Anne's, Sir Arthur continued to be a partner with his brother Edward Cecil in the brewery business, but over the years, he showed a declining interest in the active management of the business. It was well known that Lady Olive, his wife, was not happy about his connection with the brewery trade, but at the same time it provided them with a large income. In 1876 when the original deed of partnership came up for renewal, Edward Cecil proposed that its terms be revised to reflect the imbalance between the brothers in the management of the business. Sir Arthur had limited business experience and his periodic intrusions into the management of the brewery often irritated his younger brother, who showed exceptional business acumen despite his young years. For the eight years since their father's death in 1868, the profits at the brewery soared and amounted to £1,500,000.

Sir Arthur was unwilling to give up a partnership that had yielded him a personal income of £530,000 over these eight years, especially on the terms of his father's will, which stated that the retiring partner would only get £30,000. A new agreement was drawn up and signed in August 1876 that would have permitted the retiring partner to get compensation of almost £484,000, which was a more accurate reflection of the business at this time. This new agreement was only effective for two months, because on 12 October 1876, the partnership was finally dissolved on very favourable terms. Sir Arthur received £600,000 for his share of the business, plus £80,000, as his share of the profits for 1876. The total sum of £680,000 was to be paid over four years in six instalments, with the first payment due on 1 January 1877. Although Sir Arthur received more than was envisaged under Sir Benjamin Lee's will, the main object of the will had been achieved. The brewery was kept intact and under the control of a single proprietor. Sir Arthur was now a very rich man and this retirement sum, together with his many other investments, left him free for his real interests, public life and philanthropy. A general election had been called in 1874, and Sir Arthur again stood as a Conservative and Unionist candidate for Parliament and regained his seat, which he held until 1880.[19]

CHAPTER EIGHT

Acquisitions: 1876–1878

On 2 November 1876, just two months after retiring from the brewery with his golden handshake, Sir Arthur obtained two leases from the Barlow family for their house and lands in Sybil Hill townland, in Clontarf Parish, the border of which was close to the now expanded St Anne's. Sybil Hill, a Georgian house and its land, had been in the Barlow family for a very long time, but when John Barlow, a magistrate, died in January 1876,[1] his son and family were willing to sell their leases and move elsewhere. The first lease was for the house and 36 acres, and referred to the original lease of 20 January 1732 from John Vernon of Clontarf, which was for a term of 999 years at the yearly rent of £40. Sir Arthur paid £5,000 to James Thomas Barlow and his eldest son, John Herbert Ralph Barlow, for this lease.[2] The second lease was for 17 acres and referred to an earlier lease of 16 April 1746 from John Vernon to John Barlow and a renewal lease of 30 January 1845, which were now held by James Thomas Barlow. This lease, which Sir Arthur now took over, was for a period of 41 years from 1 November 1876, paying a yearly rent of £75-12-0 to James Thomas Barlow.[3]

Just over a year later, in February 1878, Sir Arthur obtained the last part of the Raheny land in Maryville townland, which was now wedged between St Anne's estate and Sybil Hill lands. Another Georgian house, Maryville, built in the late eighteenth century, was situated close to Sybil Hill, and had been in lease also to the Barlow family by 1848, according to the Valuation Books. Over the years, the Barlow family let the house and land to different tenants, but now relinquished the lease. Sir Arthur leased Maryville House with 63 acres from the Earl of Howth, with the consent of the mortgagee of the premises, which was still the Represen-

St Anne's: The Story of a Guinness Estate

Maryville House added to St Anne's estate in 1878. *M. Milne.*

tative Body of the Church of Ireland, for a period of 500 years from 1 November 1877. The yearly rent was £354-9-9, with a stipulation that this would increase to £446-12-0 after the death of the Earl of Howth and Sir Arthur.[4] From the Valuation Books and *Thom's Directories,* both Sybil Hill house and Maryville house were vacant for a while, but by 1881 Walter Keating, Sir Arthur's private secretary, was living in Sybil Hill. Maryville house was also later used as a residence for the land steward and other workers at St Anne's estate.

This was the last lease acquired by Sir Arthur and brought the total area of the St Anne's estate to just under 500 acres. An interesting fact emerges from checking the total area covered by the estate in the Valuation Books and the corresponding maps. All the land on the south side of the Howth Road from the entrance to Sybil Hill up to Raheny Village was now part of St Anne's estate, except for one field of only five acres. It was situated in the townland of Harmonstown in Clontarf parish, beside the gate lodge to Maryville house, and next to the Raheny glebe land of six acres bought by Sir Arthur in 1875. Down through all the following years, it is shown on all the Valuation Books as occupied and owned by the Vernon family of Clontarf Castle. It never became part of St Anne's estate and this piece of land stands out very significantly when looking at the maps. It seems likely that Sir Arthur would have wanted to acquire this field, as it was now wedged between all his land, but for whatever reason, Vernon never leased it to him or anyone else, and what it was used for during these years is not known.

CHAPTER NINE

House, Grounds and New Buildings

In about 1873, Sir Arthur commissioned the architect James Franklin Fuller to plan and supervise the remodelling of his house at St Anne's, almost doubling it in size, with Thomas Millard as builder.[1] Clearly, Sir Arthur spent a lot of time and money on upgrading the house, which incorporated part of the old Thornhill house as well as the first St Ann's house. Some rooms were built at angles to get the most of the lovely views over Dublin Bay. It took about seven years to complete.

Apparently Sir Arthur and Fuller had a disagreement, and another architect, George Coppinger Ashlin, was entrusted with completing the house. It was described as the 'most palatial house built in Ireland during the second half of the 19th century', and was comparable to the mansions of that period being built in the USA by people such as the Vanderbilts.[2] The two-storey exterior of the mansion kept its Italianate character and was carried out in Bath and Portland stone, with a single-storey front entrance portico. The interior included the main hall, often used as a ballroom, with a gallery supported by Ionic marble columns reached by a vast double staircase of marble in the Renaissance style. The dining room had a mantelpiece of handsomely carved wood, and led to the large conservatory at the rear, which had a marble floor and a domed roof with cupola. The drawing room with ornate plasterwork in the coved ceiling and an organ in the apse, so admired by Frederick Ogilby in the original house of Benjamin Lee, was retained in this remodelling.

One of the most interesting new features was a winter garden in the centre of the mansion, called a palm court, with a glass roof. It adjoined the main hall and upper gallery, and measured 66 feet by 38 feet (21.1 metres by 11.5 metres). There was also a statue room with a fine emblem-

Front view of St Anne's house taken at a garden party in 1912. *Gillman collection, IAA.*

atic ceiling, and a picture room with a Bossi mantelpiece, all built to house the growing collection of works of art. Upstairs, the boudoir was a charming room with a panelled oak dado, a beautifully carved wooden mantelpiece, a ceiling and door heavily ornamented with gilt finishing, and windows facing south opening on to a large balcony, with views overlooking Dublin Bay.[3] It was during this remodelling that the Roman tower on the roof was removed and resited on a mound overlooking the lake,[4] and also the Georgian door-case of the original house erected as an entrance to a French lavender garden.[5]

To complement their new house at St Anne's, Sir Arthur and Lady Olivia now turned their energy to the grounds of the estate. They greatly admired French houses and gardens, and this influence was seen at St Anne's when they laid out grand *allées* radiating from the house. A new main avenue was laid out westwards from the house, which ran in a straight line one mile long and was flanked on either side by alternative plantings of the evergreen Holm Oak and Austrian Pine. Sir Arthur and his wife were lovers of trees and they planted great belts of the Holm Oak along the boundaries of the estate to give shelter from the easterly gales and the salt sea air. A sport of the rose 'Souvenir de la Malmaison' from the Chateau de Malmaison, home of Empress Josephine, was discovered at St Anne's by the head gardener, Andrew Campbell, and named 'Souvenir de St Anne's'. It is still grown today in the Rose Garden. A plant propagated at St Anne's, the red *Lobelia cardinalis,* was named 'The Bishop' after Sir Arthur's nephew, Bishop Benjamin Plunket.

When Sir Arthur acquired all the Raheny lands in 1874, it also included a by-road called Wade's Lane that is clearly marked on the first Ordnance Survey map of 1837. This by-road started at Watermill Road and was the boundary between the townlands of Raheny South, Bettyville and Charleville, passing the house of Brighton Lodge and emerging at Blackbush Lane. It was a short cut for Raheny people to get to Clontarf. The new main avenue, which Sir Arthur proposed to lay out from his new mansion, now cut across Wade's Lane and caused a problem for him as local people were still entitled to use this 'right-of-way'. He overcame this problem and preserved his privacy by constructing a tunnel under the main avenue to facilitate local people, while also preventing them being seen by him as they crossed the main avenue of his estate.[6] The tunnel is marked on the 1907 Ordnance Survey Map. Sir Arthur would have liked this tree-lined avenue to run straight to the Howth Road, thus giving a complete straight vista to his new mansion, but the lands of Furry Park estate blocked his way. It is reported that the owner, Sir Ralph Smith Cusack, would not sell the land to him. Therefore the new main avenue of St Anne's estate had to turn to the right to exit onto the Howth Road and joined the entrance to Sybil Hill house. Later a new entrance and gate lodge were built on the other side of Sybil Hill house at the western boundary of the estate, which connected to the new long main avenue.

While all this work was going on at St Anne's, Sir Arthur also found time to spend his money on many other projects. He continued his father's generosity towards public works, and together with his brother Edward funded the Dublin Exhibition of 1872, which boosted the busi-

Clock Tower, *view facing west from inside the walled garden. This four-storey brick tower was built c. 1854 by Benjamin Lee Guinness. Photo: Dublin City Council.*

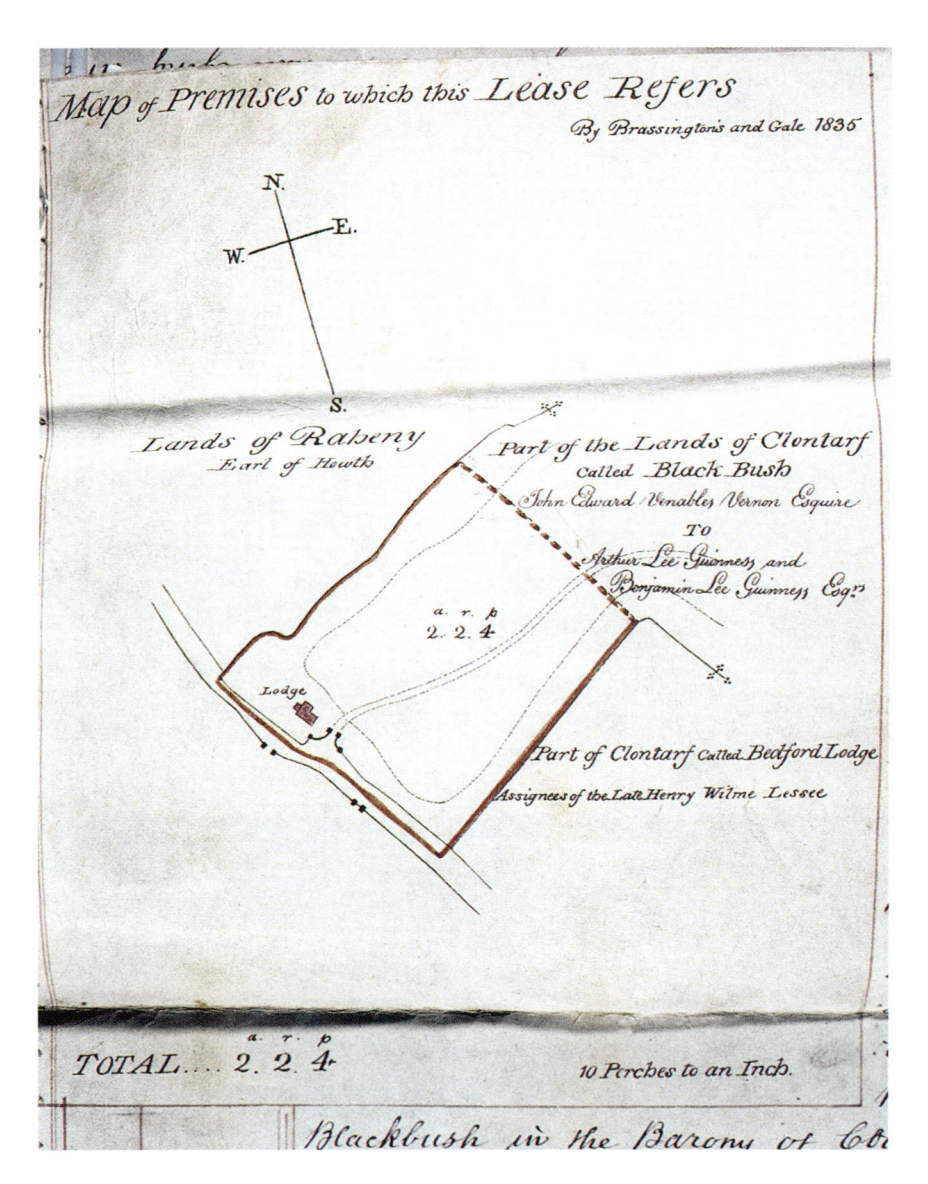

*Brassington and Gale's **1835 Map of the Upper Meadow**, adjoining Thornhill estate with entrance from Blackbush Lane, now Mount Prospect Avenue. Photography by David Davison and Associates from the original deed held by Dublin City Council.*

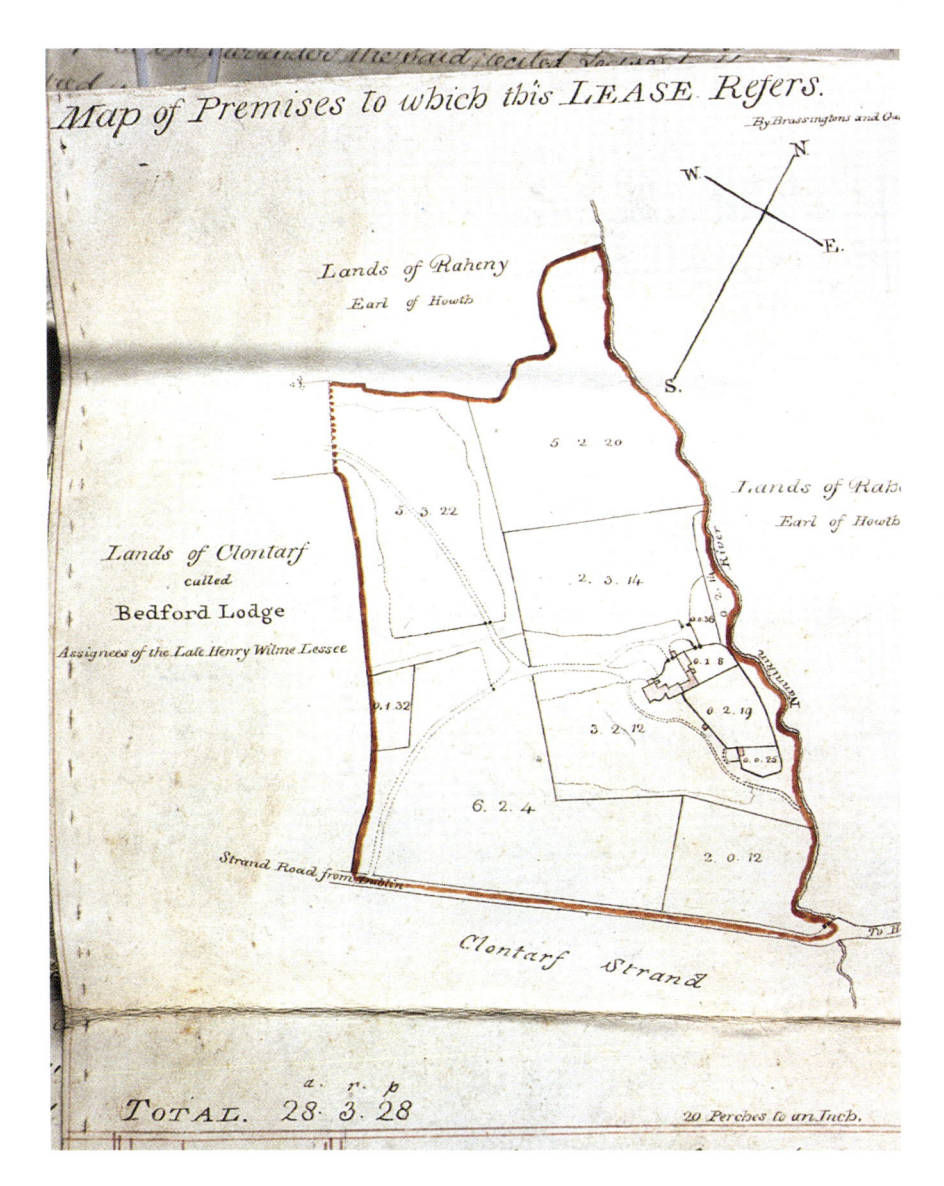

Brassington and Gale's **1835 Map of Thornhill House and Estate**, with entrance from coast road, now James Larkin Road. Photography by David Davison and Associates from the original deed held by Dublin City Council.

Sealawn Lodge at original entrance to the estate on the coast road. Photo: Goodbody.

Close up view of Clock Tower facing east showing details of the Booth clock and figures. Photo: Martin McChree.

All Saints' Lodge. *Former gate lodge at Raheny entrance to St. Anne's, later used as sexton's residence. Photo: J. Sharkey.*

Crest *over entrance door to **All Saint's Lodge** showing Lord and Lady Ardilaun's initials intertwined beneath a crown. Photo: J. Sharkey.*

Aerial view of Rose Garden, with Red Stables beyond and the tree lined main avenue to the left. Photo: Dublin City Council.

View of **Clock and Cupola**.
Photo: J. Sharkey.

Lamp *on entrance pillar gate.*
Photo: J. Sharkey.

Detail of **Window**. *Photo: J. Sharkey.*

View of the former tree-lined **Church Walk** *from St. Anne's to All Saints' Church, preserved today amid the modern housing estate built by Dublin Corporation. Photo: J. Sharkey.*

Rear and side view of house with conservatory. *Gillman collection, IAA.*

ness life of the city. After his retirement from the brewery, Sir Arthur gave the impression of 'giving money away not to please others but to please himself. In his choice of objects for his munificence he showed imagination and an unconventional sense of discrimination.'[7] He continued the work his father had commenced re-constructing Archbishop Marsh's Library near St Patrick's Cathedral, while also clearing the slums in that area. He became chairman of the first Dublin organisation concerned with housing of artisans. He rebuilt the Coombe Lying-in Hospital and served for 16 years as President of the Royal Dublin Society, while also financing the publication of a history of the society.

His biggest project was acquiring the then private park of St Stephen's Green from all the keyholders and turning it into a public park for the people of Dublin. In 1877 the St Stephen's Green (Dublin) Act was passed at Westminster to facilitate the re-opening. Sir Arthur personally spent £20,000 on landscaping the park with walks, flowerbeds and an ornamental lake, and it opened to the public without ceremony on 27 July 1880.[8]

His many acts of generosity to his native city were rewarded when he was raised to the peerage and took his seat in the House of Lords.[9] He took the name, Ardilaun, *ard oileán,* meaning 'high island', after the name of the island in Lough Corrib on his Ashford estate.[10] This was the first peerage to be bestowed on a member of the Guinness family. He could now add the crown to his coat of arms, and his family's motto, *Spes mea in Deo,* to the pediment which adorned the new St Anne's house. By 1882, he had disposed of his interest in his town house, Number 18 Leeson Street, and it became a convent belonging to the Sacred Heart Order. In 1892, Dublin Corporation erected a statue of Lord Ardilaun, by the sculptor Thomas Farrell, in St Stephen's Green, as a token of appreciation for his munificence to his native city.[11]

As previously related, Lord Ardilaun had the rights of presentation to the Raheny Church of Ireland Parish. In 1881 he made a proposal to build a new church for the parish, at his own expense, on a site in St Anne's estate, near Raheny village. This was to replace the old church of St Assam, which was built in 1609, then rebuilt in 1712, but was now falling into disrepair. The parishioners gratefully accepted his offer.[12] A

St Stephen's Green Park bought by Sir Arthur Guinness in 1876, remodelled and landscaped to open as a public park on 27 July 1880. *S. Kerins collection.*

very generous offer, it also greatly enhanced his position, as few of the landed gentry of that time could boast of having their own private church on their estates. But in the years ahead, it was the Raheny parishioners who benefited from his generosity. Although it was privately built, the church was open to all parishioners and was administered according to rules and traditions of the Church of Ireland. The architect George Ashlin, who was finishing the remodelling of the mansion, was also engaged by Lord Ardilaun to design the new church. It was built by Messrs Collen Brothers of Dublin and Portadown, and was completed by 1889 at a personal cost to Lord Ardilaun of £9,000.[13]

The building of the church caused much interest and comment in newspapers and periodicals over the course of its construction. *The Irish Builder* had many articles about the church, but strangely never once referred to the rebuilding of St Anne's house. The general symmetry of the proportions of the new church, as well as its perfection of detail, was much admired. It was designed in the Early English style, the outer walls built of granite, with limestone dressings and the roof covered with Westmoreland green slates, while the steeple was modelled on that at Salisbury Cathedral. Internally the walls were lined with Bath stone, with Irish marble shafts, while the roof was of panelled pitch pine and the floor was in wood block and ceramic mosaic.[14] The new church was called All Saints', in memory of his father, Sir Benjamin Lee, who was born on All Saints' Day, 1 November, as also was Lord Ardilaun himself. The dedication of the Church was set for All Saints' Day in 1889, but was postponed due to the death of Lord Ardilaun's sister, Lady Anne Plunket, wife of the Archbishop of Dublin. The dedication took place a few weeks later on 16 December. The church could not be consecrated at this time, as the rule of the Church only permits consecration on freehold land, and the ground on which the church was built was held in lease from Lord Howth. Lord Ardilaun also gave an undertaking to maintain the old Church of St Assam's and graveyard while also meeting all expenses for the new church.[15] Later, a new tree-lined avenue was also laid out from St Anne's house to the new church.

At the same time as the new church was being built, Lord Ardilaun also started another building project on St Anne's estate. He used the

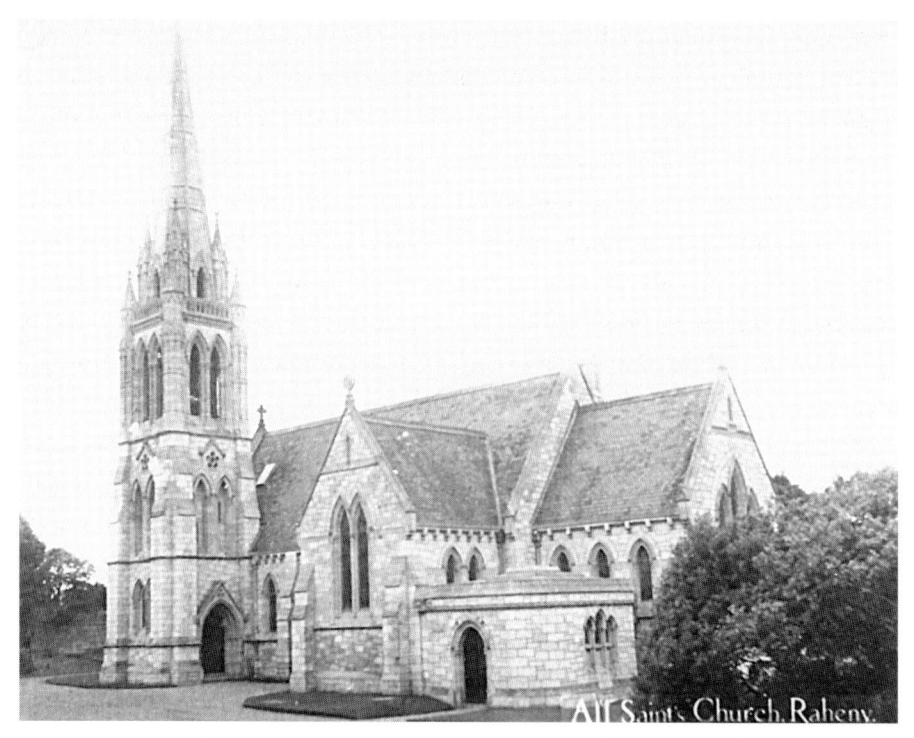

All Saints' Church Raheny which opened in 1889. *Courtesy of the National Library, WR 2035.*

same architect, George Ashlin, and the same contractors, Collen Brothers, to build new stables on a site near Bedford Lodge in 1885. These Tudor-style stables stood on three sides of a quadrangle 150 feet (45.7 metres) square and built of ornamental Portmarnock red brick, with a striking cupola above, and cost £6,000.[16] These beautiful stables are known today as the Red Stables and are enclosed within iron gates and railings. When completed, the Red Stables were rated at £50 by the Valuation Office, while the new St Anne's house increased its valuation from £107-15-0 to £600 when finally rated in February 1882.

While Lord Ardilaun was spending his money and energy on developing St Anne's into a fitting estate for his elevated social position, his younger brother, Edward Cecil, was also gaining social distinction for himself, as well as immersing himself in the further expansion and development of the brewery. In 1873, Edward had married his second cousin,

Adelaide Guinness, and also acquired a country house outside Dublin, called Farmleigh, with 60 acre stretching from the Phoenix Park to Castleknock.[17] Edward engaged the same architect as his brother Arthur, James Franklin Fuller, to extend his new house, where he and his wife entertained lavishly, as well as at the town house in St Stephen's Green. The two Guinness brothers and their wives became the leaders of society in Dublin, and later also in London. In 1885, Edward was given a baronetcy, in recognition of his 'high position in Ireland' as well as his 'services rendered' during the state visit to Dublin of the Prince and Princess of Wales.[18] The brewery was thriving under his management and in 1886, just ten years after the dissolution of the partnership between Arthur and Edward, the brewery was turned into a limited company and sold to the public for £6 million. Sir Edward became an extremely wealthy man, while still maintaining control as chairman of the new company.[19]

The other Guinness brother, Captain Benjamin Lee of the Royal Horse Guards, married Lady Henrietta St Lawrence, daughter of the late third Earl of Howth and sister of the fourth Earl, on 6 September 1881.[20] This marriage strengthened closer ties between the two families, and Lord Ardilaun was now a brother-in-law to Lord Howth, his neighbour and landlord in north Dublin.

The main hall with gallery above supported by marble columns. *Plunket collection.*

Landing and upper section of the marble staircase. *Plunket collection.*

Drawing Room with coved ceiling and organ in apse, part of first St Ann's house built by Benjamin Lee Guinness. *Plunket collection.*

Drawing Room facing opposite direction and showing less furniture. *Gillman collection.*

Dining Room leading to the large conservatory. *Gillman collection, IAA.*

Lady Ardilaun's boudoir leading to balcony with views over the sea. *Plunket collection.*

CHAPTER TEN

More Land Dealings

Although Lord Ardilaun poured money over the years into developing his St Anne's estate into a fine mansion and demesne, it is reported that he also spent a vast amount, almost £2 million, on turning his Ashford estate in Mayo into a massive baronial castle and estate. Building work on the Ashford house continued all during his life and he was constantly adding practical improvements, from generating his own electricity from the lake to building 25 miles of roads around the estate, which were wide enough for the new horseless carriages. He also kept a yacht, 'The Eglinton', on the lake beside Ashford. By 1880 he had planted over one million trees on 3,000 acres and developed the woodcock shooting into the best in Europe, culminating with the historic shoot in 1905 of the Prince of Wales, soon to be King George V.[1]

It seemed that the two Guinness estates differed greatly with each other in many aspects. St Anne's had become an estate of just less than 500 acres, situated close to Dublin City, with originally only a small number of tenants with yearly leases. As discussed earlier, Sir Arthur took over their tenancies when their leases expired, to become sole occupier of the land, with only one tenant, Anthony O'Toole, objecting to his lease not being renewed. St Anne's was then developed into a compact estate over which Sir Arthur had total control. On the other hand, the Ashford estate covered a vast area situated in the wild beauty of Connemara, which Sir Arthur had inherited from his father. The Galway estate comprised 19,944 acres, with 3,266 acres in Mayo, centred in the parishes of Cong and Clonbur. There were 670 tenants on the estate and most of the farms were between 15 and 25 acres with rents ranging from 5/- to 40/- an acre. Sir Arthur employed about 400 labourers and artisans in the exten-

Ashford Castle, Cong, Co. Mayo. The old Oranmore and Brown house can be seen on the right with later additions by Lord Ardilaun on the left. *Courtesy of the National Library of Ireland VR 2883.*

sion and maintenance of Ashford Castle alone. He was regarded as an improving landlord, expending large amount of money on drainage, pier construction, cottage construction, and other tasks, which generated much employment and greatly improved the circumstances of his tenants. But his relationship with his tenants was strained during the Land League's agitation in the west in 1879–1880.

Sir Arthur was a Conservative MP for Dublin with a simplistic attitude to maintaining the *status quo* and he was outraged by the Land League's action in the area. Sir Arthur was the only person who stood up against the League by giving support to Captain Charles Boycott, a land agent who was ostracised on an estate nearby in Co. Mayo. Gerald Moran in his essay, 'Landlord and Tenant Relations in Ireland', gives us a detailed insight into Sir Arthur's relationship with his own tenants on the Ashford estate during this difficult period. Moran stated that the one issue which created bad feeling between landlord and tenant was zealous prosecutions for trespass on Ashford woods and lakes, which Guinness stocked for fishing and shooting. Moran states that:

> while Guinness enjoyed a good rapport with his tenants, he was determined to exercise a strong hand against those tenants who had the potential to cause trouble. He wanted an estate where all could share the benefits of his improvements. However as with all such developments there are winners and losers.

Guinness opposed the Land League's intimidation tactics against the payment of rents. Most of his tenants were in a position to pay their rents but were told to withhold them. When they looked for rent reduction, he at first refused, but by December 1879 he consented to a rent abatement of between 20 and 30 per cent for most of his smaller tenants. Moran states that Guinness was renowned for his charity to his tenants, donating £3,000 for the purchase of meal during major distress in 1879, and as most of them were Catholics, he gave financial support for Catholic churches and schools in the area. His legacy must be seen in the light of the improved circumstances it brought to most of the people of his western estates. The demise of the Land League after 1882 helped to partially restore the relationship between Guinness and his tenants in Cong. But he was aware that life would never be the same again, and 'he was one of the first landlords in Mayo to sell off his estate to his tenants under the terms of the 1885 Ashbourne Land Act.'[2]

No similar tenant problems occurred at St Anne's estate. It was now a beautiful demesne of under 500 acres, but whenever any opportunity arose to acquire other lands in the area, Lord Ardilaun always seemed to step forward and spend his money. Ownership of North Bull Island along the coastline originated in a royal charter granted by Charles II to the Vernon estate, relating to tidal flats and sections of the sea shore on the north side of Dublin Bay.[3] When Griffith's Valuation was published in 1848, the area of the North Bull Island in Clontarf Parish consisted of 100 acres of sandbank in fee to the Vernon family, with a strip of land of 10 acres along the North Bull Wall in fee to the Ballast Board. The eastern part, called the North Bull Islands, was in Raheny Parish, and was only six acres of sandbank in fee to the Earl of Howth. The two separate islands kept growing and formed into one island.

After 1868 the Valuation Cancelled Books recorded the Clontarf section as 230 acres, while the Raheny section grew rapidly to 144 acres, which by 1914 had increased to 355 acres. Initially Lord Ardilaun leased only two acres of the North Bull Island opposite St Anne's estate from the Earl of Howth, for a term of 99 years from 1 November 1890 at a yearly rent of ten shillings.[4] Then in July 1894 Lord Ardilaun bought the remainder of the east section of the North Bull Island from the Earl of Howth for £2,000, with the consent of the Representative Church Body as mortgagee and of Julian Gaisford, the nephew and heir of the Earl of Howth. This covered an area from the Naniken River at St Anne's estate, along the shore to Kilbarrack Cottage, across the island and seashore to the Martello Tower at Sutton and finishing at a headland on Howth Head.

The Earl of Howth reserved the right to ride on the island. A mortgage, dated the same day, stated that this land at North Bull Island would revert back to the Earl of Howth, if at any time up to the 31 December 1903 Lord Ardilaun was evicted by the crown from any part of the purchased land of North Bull. In that event the Earl of Howth would repay the purchased price as well as interest at five per cent per annum to Lord Ardilaun. The reason the Earl of Howth had his clause written into the mortgage agreement was that he stated he had no legal evidence to prove his title to Bull Island 'as to bar all crown rights', even though his family had possession for over 60 years. Obviously Howth felt he needed to safeguard his own interest, as well as Lord Ardilaun's acquisition of the island, for the next ten years.[5]

Adjacent to St Anne's was another estate, Baymount Castle, and its 20 acres stretched from Blackbush Lane down to the sea in Heronstown townland. This castellated Georgian house, originally called Granby Hill, had been the residence of the Church of Ireland Bishop of Down and Connor, Dr Trail. The Vernon family leased it to John Kiely from 20 March 1834 for 99 years at the yearly rent of £113-7-8 and then to Robert Warren from 8 October 1842 for 110 years. In 1845, the Loreto

More Land Dealings

BAYMOUNT SCHOOL, DOLLYMOUNT.

PREPARATORY FOR THE PUBLIC SCHOOLS AND ROYAL NAVY.

prospectus apply
W. LUCAS SCOTT, M.A.

Baymount Castle acquired by Lord Ardilaun in 1898 where he later established Baymount School. *S. Kerins collection.*

Order of nuns, under its foundress Mother Ball, opened a school at Baymount, but after a disastrous fire in 1851, it moved out to Balbriggan, Co. Dublin. A businessman, George Tickell, then acquired the property. In March 1898, Lord Ardilaun paid £2,000 to Adelaide Tickell, the widow of George Tickell, with the consent of Edward Vernon as landlord, for the remainder of the original leases of 1834 and 1842, paying the same yearly rent of £113-7-8.[6] A few years later, Lord Ardilaun established Baymount School. It was a preparatory boys' school for the English public schools and for the Royal Navy, and William Lucas Scott was appointed as the head master. He leased the school and land from Lord Ardilaun for a term of 21 years from 1 August 1904 paying a yearly rent of £200.[7] The school continued for over 40 years, and for many years the pupils took part in the Sunday choir service in All Saints' Church, Raheny.

By 1900 the lease on the 17 acres of Sybil Hill land, adjacent to Vernon Avenue in Clontarf, was due to expire, and Lord Ardilaun secured a new long lease for this land from Edward Vernon of Clontarf Castle. The lease was for a term of 250 years from 29 September 1898 at the yearly

Tram coming, Howth at Dollymount, Dublin.

The Clontarf to Howth tram showing the single line track along St Anne's estate. *S. Kerins collection.*

rent of £260-15-6. A covenant stated that Lord Ardilaun was to expend £2,000 within five years on building two or more villas on this land, but in fact no buildings were ever erected, thus incurring a rent penalty.[8]

The Ardilauns enjoyed their privacy on St Anne's estate and were not pleased with the plans of the Clontarf and Hill of Howth Tramshed Company Ltd, established in 1898, to run an electric tram line from Clontarf to Howth along the edge of their estate at St Anne's. The company acquired two acres, two roods and 34 perches of land of the estate in the townlands of Heronstown and Bettyville to lay the tram lines.[9] The tramline opened in July 1900, only after the company agreed to the strict conditions imposed by Lord Ardilaun. This included free access for him to the foreshore and his rifle range on North Bull Island, non-interference with the free flow of the Naniken and Santry Rivers, and a single track only to be laid along the St Anne's section of the tramline, with no passengers allowed to set down along this section.[10] The trams made accessible the whole area, from the city centre all the way to Howth, and were commercially and socially very successful.

More Land Dealings

In April 1900, just a few months before the trams came into operation, a very important visitor travelled along the Clontarf Road. It was the now elderly Queen Victoria on her last state visit to Ireland. Among her many engagements during her stay, she found time one afternoon to visit Lord and Lady Ardilaun at St Anne's. The *Irish Times* of 20 April described the afternoon drive by the Queen to St Anne's. It reported that she entered the estate by the avenue from the coast road, under the Annie Lee tower bridge, and was met at the entrance porch to the house by Lady Ardilaun, who presented her with a 'bouquet of yellow primroses'. The Queen departed down the long avenue, where 'numerous groups of Lord Ardilaun's employees gave the Royal party a cheery send-off', and emerged from the estate at the Howth Road near Sybil Hill, to return to the city.[11]

Lord Ardilaun's final acquisition of land in the area was in July 1902, when he bought a major part of the western half of North Bull Island, situated in Clontarf Parish, for £3,000, in fee simple. The land was sold by Edward Vernon of Clontarf Castle under the Landed Estates Court and covered an area of 922 acres including the adjacent foreshore. The rights of the public to walk the lands and bathe from the foreshore, as well as the exclusive rights of the Royal Dublin Golf Club to play golf, were written into the sale agreement.

The Royal Dublin Golf Club had been founded in 1885 as the Dublin Golf Club, with a course laid out in the Phoenix Park. The club moved to Sutton for three years, and then in 1889 secured permission from Edward Vernon to play golf on a section of his land on North Bull island for two years and then from year to year. In 1891, the club changed its name to the Royal Dublin Golf Club and the following year secured a lease from Edward Vernon for its members to exclusively play golf on the island, for a term of 21 years from 21 December 1892, paying £20 rent per annum.[12] Following Lord Ardilaun's acquisition of the major portion of the island in 1902, the trustees of Royal Dublin Golf Club, on 16 December 1903, also bought 144 acres of the island and foreshore in Clontarf parish, in fee simple from the Landed Estates Court for £400.[13] The golf club further extended its course on the island when Lord Ardilaun granted the club a lease on 21 May 1904 on his part of the

St Anne's: The Story of a Guinness Estate

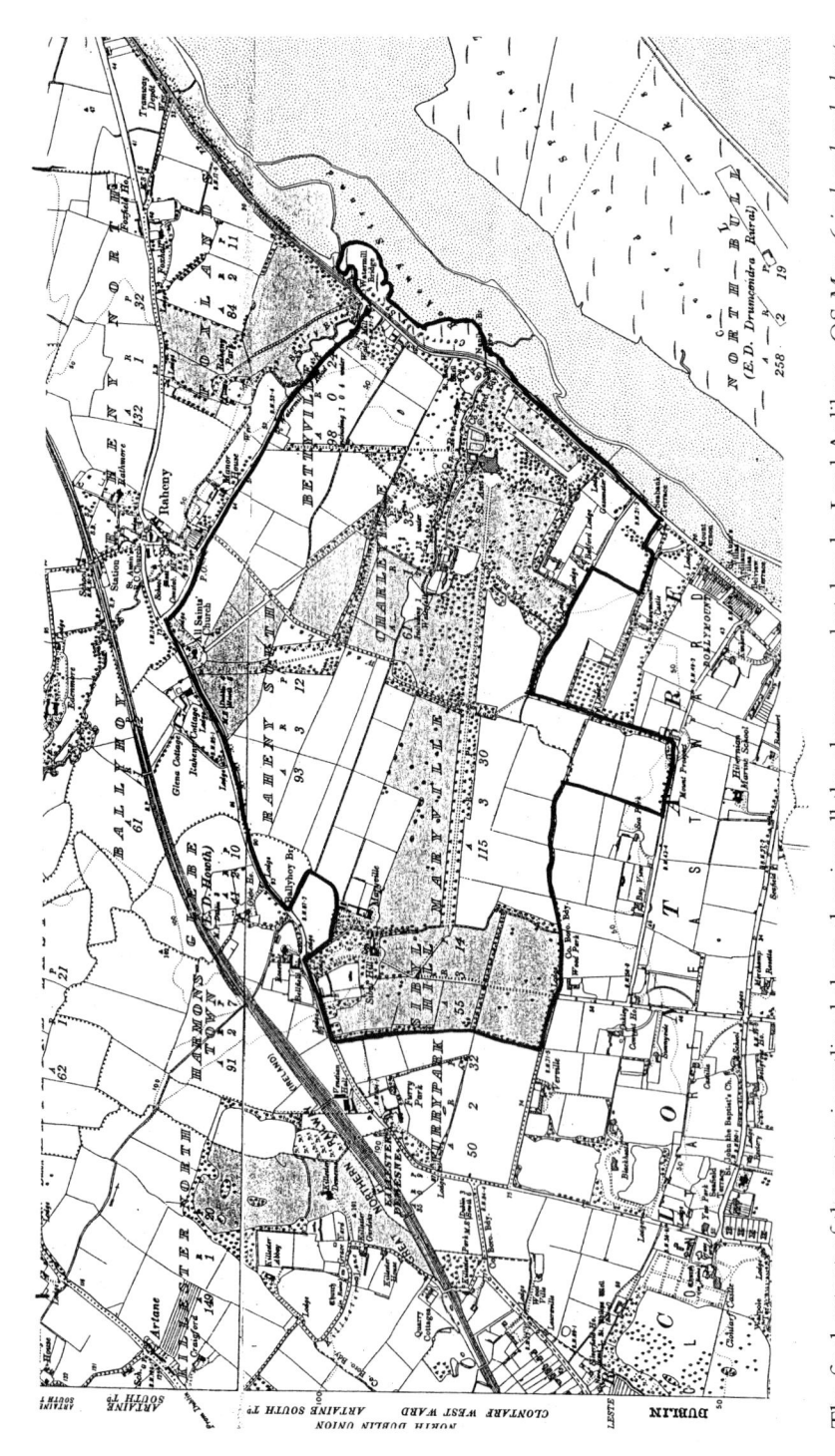

The final extent of the estate is outlined above showing all the changes undertaken by Lord Ardilaun. OS Map, 6 inch reduced, sheets 15 & 19, revised 1907.

island. This lease gave the club the right to play golf from the boundary of the club's land to the eastern extremity of the island, for a period of 21 years subject to a yearly rent of £200.[14]

With his ownership of most of North Bull Island, as well as his own estate at St Anne's, and Baymount Castle, Lord Ardilaun now held a substantial amount of land in north Dublin that almost equalled that held by his two landlords, Vernon and Howth. Nor was his interest in land acquisitions confined to Dublin. The Muckross estate, which included the Lakes of Killarney, was put up for auction in 1899 and created huge interest in Ireland as well as in America. The estate did not sell at the auction and the sale was adjourned. Later it was announced that Lord Ardilaun had purchased the estate for £60,000. It is generally believed that he bought it to save it from commercial development and also at the instigation of his wife Olive, who was a niece of the former owner, Henry Arthur Herbert. The Ardilauns did not spend much time there and eventually sold it in 1911, to Mr Bowers Bourn who bought it as a wedding present for his daughter Maud Vincent. The Vincent family later handed the estate to the Irish nation and it became Ireland's first national park.[15]

Lord Ardilaun took his politics very seriously and all his life he was a confirmed Unionist, believing that Unionism would serve the best interest of Ireland. In his later years, to ensure a platform for his opposition to Home Rule and the Land League, as well as to express his frustration with all politicians during these years, he bought four Dublin newspapers, *Daily Express, Morning Mail, Evening Mail* and *Weekly Warden*.[16] Although his parliamentary duties necessitated him spending long periods in London, he also spent considerable time and energy attending to his two estates, St Anne's and Ashford, as well as his many business interests in Dublin.

He led an active life up to shortly before his death on 20 January 1915 at St Anne's in his seventy-fifth year. He was buried in his mortuary chapel of All Saints' Church, Raheny. His obituary in the *Irish Times* stated that he had continued the family tradition of giving service and all his life had played an enthusiastic part in the public life of his native city. 'As a philanthropist he knew no politics.' If an undertaking demanded his sympathy and support, it had it, whether it was for Nationalist or Unionist, Roman Catholic or Protestant, as long as 'the cause was good.'[17] Lord and Lady Ardilaun had a long and happy marriage but had no children. The peerage and Ardilaun title became extinct, having no son to inherit, and the baronetcy he inherited from his father, Sir Benjamin Lee, passed to his nephew, Algernon Arthur Guinness, eldest son of his late brother, Captain Benjamin Guinness. His will stated that the management of the Ashford estate 'would impose too much care on my darling wife and with her concurrence' that estate was therefore bequeathed to his brother Edward Cecil, who in 1891 had become Lord Iveagh, and now was Viscount Iveagh. Lady Ardilaun inherited St Anne's, including North Bull Island and Baymount, the right of presentation of a Rector for All Saints' Church, Raheny, two houses in St Stephen's Green, and the London house at Carlton Terrace. His estate was valued at £495,638.[18]

The probate documents of his will give some insight into St Anne's estate and, in the absence of any estate records, are the only evidence that show a large part of the estate was still extensively farmed apart from the pleasure gardens and demesne.

In the month following Lord Ardilaun's death, his executors instructed the firm of Gavin Low Ltd to hold a public auction for the letting of the lands for the year, as well as holding an extensive clearance sale at Maryville, Raheny. The reason the lands were let so soon after Lord Ardilaun's death was to give the valuers a definite open market value on which to base their valuation for probate and estate duties. The advertisement on 6 February 1915 in the *Irish Times* for the farm clearance auction listed quite an amount of livestock, crops and farm machinery. It included: 40 cattle, 130 sheep, eight horses, 130 tons of hay, 42 tons of straw, 40 tons of turnips, 20 tons of potatoes, 80 barrels of wheat, 150 barrels of oats and 50 tons of manure. The letting of the lands of St Anne's and Maryville was for 114 Irish acres in divisions of three to 30 acres for grazing: 16 acres for oats and 10 acres for root crop with farmyard manure supplied.

Messrs Stopford & Turner, the valuers for St Anne's estate, produced their report on 9 March 1915. The report shows that the value of the livestock and crops sold at auction amounted to £2,602-13-6. The auction sale for letting the land had achieved a full letting with a rental of £3-10-0 per acre, with the executors responsible for payment of head rent and all rates, and the maintenance of fences and watering of stock. As a large area within the estate had no natural surface water supply, water would have to be carried through for all stock, and therefore 20 shillings per acre was deducted from the rental, giving a net amount of £2-10-0 per acre.

The most interesting and amazing aspect of the report was the observations about the value of the whole estate. The valuers felt it was impossible to put a value on the estate, as it was held under different leases and subject to very high rents, total annual rents amounted to £2,213-0-4. St Anne's estate with gardens and demesne entailed a very large outlay for maintenance, at that time employing 22 men full time. The report stated that only a very rich man could afford to maintain the upkeep of the demesne and 'if it was on the market it would we consider be impossible to find a purchaser.' For valuation purposes, as 'there was no demand for building ground in the locality,' the land was dealt with by the valuers 'from an agricultural standpoint only.' The lands of North Bull Island and Baymount were included in the assessment. The report concluded that the fee simple valuation of the entire property was £40,888, the capital value of head rents and tithe rent charges was £51,660, the cost of abolishing all the ornamental avenues and replacing boundary fences was £2,000, which left 'a minus value of £12,772,' on the entire property.[19]

CHAPTER ELEVEN

The Twilight Years

St Anne's estate reached its peak of grandeur and prosperity during Lord Ardilaun's life, but with his death in 1915, life on the estate changed significantly. The next 20 years were a slow decline from that peak. Lord Ardilaun took an active part in the management of the estate during his lifetime, and it was intensively farmed, but this seemingly came to an end after his death, with the sale of all the livestock and crops and the farmland being rented out for the year. It seemed over the following years that the land was rented out again, and in time Lady Ardilaun decided to give leases for some of the houses on the estate.

Maryville house and three acres were leased to Mary Jane Montgomery from 1 August 1920 for 100 years paying a yearly rent of £50, as well as the Bullock yard at Maryville for 96 years from 1 August 1924 at a rent of £10.[1] Robert Kennedy married a sister of Mary Jane Montgomery and moved into Maryville House, where the family had a dairy farm for many years. Their daughter Ivy Kennedy married George Cecil Milne and he took over the lease from Mary Jane Montgomery in 1932[2] and continued to run the farm until 1945.

There were two houses at Watermill on one acre, a slated two-storey house called Watermill House and a thatched cottage. A proposal and agreement for a lease on Watermill House and cottage was signed between Lady Ardilaun and Arthur Butson, a hotel proprietor from Howth, on 8 January 1917, for a term of 70 years with a yearly rental of £20. A condition of the lease was that Arthur Butson had to spend £150 on repairs and improvements to the two houses. On 19 November 1917, Lady Ardilaun signed another proposal and agreement for a lease of a thatched cottage, called Strand Cottage, later called Coragh Cottage, situated on the coast road near Watermill House. The agreement for this lease, for a term of 99 years and yearly rent of £6, was given to Jane O'Hanlon, who owned a public house in Raheny Village. The conditions of this lease agreement were that it was to be used as a private dwelling by Jane O'Hanlon, and that she was to spend £80 on repairs to the cottage and to re-thatch the roof. In 1921, she assigned the cottage to her sister Kathleen Fennell. In later years this cottage was also called Watermill cottage, which has caused some confusion with the thatched cottage beside Watermill House leased to Arthur Butson.[3]

The old Parochial School beside the graveyard in Main Street, Raheny, bought some years ago by Lord Ardilaun, had become known as the 'Village House' and was let to various tenants over the years. On 22 May 1916, Lady Ardilaun sold the premises to the publican, Jane O'Hanlon,[4] who then sublet to other tenants over the following years. The Raheny Post Office was still in the detached red brick cottage on Watermill Road in the village. On 11 August 1922, Lady Ardilaun sold the lease of the cottage for £200 to Susan Mary Walsh, the post mistress.[5] North Bull Island had been taken over by the British military for use as a rifle range and training centre when World War One started in 1914, and the Royal Dublin Golf Club did not get possession of their links and clubhouse again until 1919. Then Lady Ardilaun gave a new lease to the club for the northern part of the island for a term of 27 years from 1 November 1919 at the yearly rent of £200.[6] A group of local residents applied to both Lady Ardilaun and Royal Dublin to form another golf club on the island. Lady Ardilaun's permission was granted on condition that her views across the island were not obscured and requested the club to be called after the estate. On 1 July 1921, St Anne's Golf Club was inaugurated, initially paying a nominal rent to Royal Dublin.[7] A formal lease was later granted by Royal Dublin to St Anne's Golf Club for a term of 20 years from 1 November 1926 at the yearly rent of £50.[8]

Lady Ardilaun was desolate and forlorn after her husband's death. In his memory, she erected an obelisk on the Ashford estate, near the shore facing the island of Ardilaun, at a place where they had spent time together and where she used to sketch and paint.[9] This obelisk commemorated Lord Ardilaun's choice of title and recalled how he subsidised a steam-

The two storey Palm Court built in the centre of the mansion adjoining the main hall. *Gillman collection, IAA.*

ship services from Galway to Cong for 24 years, until the railway line between Claremorris and Ballinrobe opened in 1892.[10] Lady Ardilaun sold the London house to a Guinness relative, as she had no need for it now. Her isolation was emphasised by now living alone in the vast mansion of St Anne's. In 1916 she invited her cousin and godchild, Katherine Olive Everett, to be her companion and secretary with the use of Sybil Hill as a home for Katherine and her two children. Katherine spent the next eight years very happily with Lady Ardilaun and in her book, *Bricks and Flowers*, gives an insight into their lives together at a time which also covered the most violent period of Irish history. These two formidable ladies shared a common love of art and gardening, but had totally different upbringings. Katherine had to earn her living and support her children when her husband left, while Lady Ardilaun had lived a sheltered life of luxury waited upon by servants all her life.

St Anne's mansion was now a very dreary place in winter. The rain often seeped through the glass roof of the winter garden and flooded the central heating. Lady Gregory described Lady Ardilaun at this time as 'a lonely figure in her wealth, childless, and feeling the old life shattered around her.[11] Katherine Everett recorded that 'for my cousin it was more like living in a mausoleum than in a home,' and whenever she got a cold, she went to stay with her maid and secretary in the Shelbourne Hotel in Dublin. Katherine, who had studied at the Slade School in London, and was an excellent interior designer and architect, was commissioned by Lady Ardilaun to convert two houses she owned in St Stephen's Green whose leases had expired into a comfortable town house. In comparison to St Anne's, it seems this town house gave Lady Ardilaun much more pleasure. During the winter months she used the house for lunch and dinner parties. The parties were socially very mixed, as officials and soldiers from Dublin Castle rubbed shoulders with artists, poets and also leaders of the emerging Sinn Féin movement. Although restrained by her aristocratic upbringing, Lady Ardilaun was radical in her support of the arts. One cannot but wonder whether or not her late husband, a staunch Unionist politician, would have approved of some of the people at these social gatherings. As a generous supporter of the Abbey Theatre, Lady Ardilaun often brought her luncheon guests to see the new Abbey plays, 'making, at Lady Gregory's request, as spectacular an entry to the theatre as possible'. This involved making several entries, going in one door and out the other side, and then around again, to attract more people to attend.[12]

Lady Ardilaun found great pleasure in her gardens and, according to Lady Gregory, this was the only reason she continued to live at St Anne's. Lady Ardilaun turned the vegetable garden into a flower garden, while she gave her cousin Katherine a free hand to also create a herb garden.[13] Garden parties were given at St Anne's during the summer, where famous figures from the world of literature, art and medicine were frequent guests. Not all of their time was spent socialising, as every week the two ladies visited many hospitals and charitable organisations throughout Dublin. Lady Ardilaun continued her late husband's support for his church, All Saints' in Raheny, by donating several beautiful stained glass windows as well as buying a new church organ. In January 1921 the male dominance of the Raheny Select Vestry was broken for the first time when Lady Ardilaun as well as her cousin Katherine Everett were elected. Both contributed much to the welfare of the parish in the following years.[14] Lady Ardilaun also visited elderly and poor residents in the village twice a year, giving presents, and one gentleman still alive has fond memories of having tea along with his Raheny school friends in St Anne's with Lady Ardilaun.[15]

Behind all their daily lives loomed the shadow of the disturbances caused by the 1916 Easter Rising leading up to the Civil War, with many murders and reprisals, as well as the looting and burning of the big houses throughout the country. Katherine was concerned about her cousin's safety and warned her not to wander around the grounds alone. She was aware that many men on the run hid in the outhouses of Sybil Hill and used the underground tunnel of the main avenue of St Anne's. In the evening after dinner, Katherine often kept her cousin company in her vast mansion, and then she would ride her bicycle down the mile-long avenue back to her own house. It was unnerving to have beams from several torches following her night ride down the avenue and on one occasion a gang of men with revolvers stopped her. She overcame her initial fear when she realised they were only young lads and after a few words were exchanged they let her pass.

Her journey to County Cork to try and discover the fate of Macroom Castle was a more daunting experience. The castle was the family home Lady Ardilaun had inherited from her father. It had been occupied first by the Black and Tans and later by the IRA, who set fire to it. Katherine went by train to Limerick, and had to get a pass from the IRA to travel the 60 miles onto Macroom, mainly using her trusty bicycle. She showed great courage and spirit in undertaking such a dangerous journey, and succeeded in rescuing much of the furniture and paintings from the burning castle. Having organised the shipment of the furniture by sea from Cork to Dublin, she then returned by bicycle and train to Dublin as quickly as possible to inform her cousin of the situation, her 'mission accomplished and the doom of Macroom Castle verified.'[16]

THE TWILIGHT YEARS

Lady Ardilaun's funeral procession with estate workers carrying wreaths from her garden, Thomas McDonnell (4th) and Peter Furey (6th) from right. *R. Daly.*

With the establishment of the Irish Free State in 1922 and the passing of the Viceregal society, the grand entertaining for which St Anne's had been built had now ceased. The death of Lady Ardilaun on 13 December 1925 at her town house, Number 42 St Stephen's Green, was really the end of an era and closed another chapter in the history of St Anne's. She was buried alongside her husband in the mortuary chapel of All Saints' Church, Raheny. Her funeral procession from St Anne's mansion through the estate to the church included all the estate workers carrying wreaths of fresh flowers from her own gardens. After her death, one old woman whom Lady Ardilaun used to visit in a tenement house described her as 'a friend to the sick and poor'.[17]

Her estate was valued at £169,366 when probate was granted initially on 27 January 1926, but corrective affidavits in November 1926 and March 1930 increased the value to £1,010,426. The Hon Benjamin J. Plunket, late Bishop of Meath, inherited St Anne's. Bishop Plunket was Lord Ardilaun's nephew, the second son of the fourth Baron Plunket and of Anne, daughter of Sir Benjamin Lee Guinness. In her will, Lady Ardilaun expressed her views about the future of St Anne's:

> In my opinion the existing house at St Anne's is far too large and expensive for anyone to live in in the future. The enormous taxation and increase of wages and cost of everything will make it impossible. I would therefore wish and advise my said nephew to dismantle the house if practicable and to build a much smaller house on the property, or to reduce the existing house to the dimension of the original house as built by Sir Benjamin Guinness.

She instructed her nephew Bishop Plunket to 'burn all my journals beginning in 1871 which are in my boudoir in St Anne's and all letters, papers, documents and Ashford visiting book.' She stated that Bishop Plunket could use his own discretion on whether to disclose or dispose of the record books 'she kept for fifty years about Lord Ardilaun and of events with which he was connected.' Regarding the right of appointment of a rector at All Saints' Church, she had very strong views and stated that 'under no circumstances is an Englishman to be appointed – any such rector must be Irish by birth and parentage'.

Bishop Plunket with family and friends in the Yew Garden. *Plunket collection.*

The Twilight Years

Her cousin Katherine Everett was left a legacy as well as the furniture she had rescued from Macroom Castle and Lady Ardilaun's diamond engagement ring. Lady Ardilaun's agent, Blayney Hamilton, was given an annuity of £800 and a lease of his Bettyville house and land for his lifetime in acknowledgement of the help in the management of her affairs 'during years of great trouble and danger'. All the members of her staff at St Anne's were given bequests and she left numerous legacies to charitable organisations, as well as a trust fund for the education for clergy to the Church of Ireland, and an endowment for history lectures in Alexandra College.[18]

When Bishop Plunket moved into St Anne's, one of his first deeds was to erect a plaque on the tower bridge in memory of his mother Annie Lee Guinness, Lord Ardilaun's sister. Bishop Plunket and his family lived at St Anne's for the next ten years and maintained the estate, even adding a walled fruit garden. The farm land continued to be let to local people. Lady Gregory wrote that Mrs Plunket was 'very anxious to do what is right for Ireland by keeping up the place, 17 labourers paid every Saturday.'[19] Bishop Plunket also carried out Lady Ardilaun's wishes by granting Blayney Hamilton a lease on his Bettyville house with 26 acres of land for his lifetime, paying a yearly rent of £50.[20] Katherine Everett left Sybil Hill and went to live in Italy for some time but later settled in England. Bishop Plunket then leased Sybil Hill house and 12 acres to Colonel Charles Newbold, the Assistant Managing Director of the Guinness brewery, for 20 years from 1 March 1928, at the yearly rent of £275.[21]

Sometime during 1932 Bishop Plunket decided to put the estate up for sale by private treaty under the joint agencies of James H North and Jackson, Stops and Joyce. The particulars of the sale described St Anne's as 'on the sea, with unequalled views, a palatial residence, with world famous gardens, lovely grounds and parkland, and also eight houses let to substantial tenants, as well as four gate lodges and six other cottages.'[22] Although an illustrated sale catalogue was printed, and presented to the National Library in November 1932, it appears the sale was not advertised extensively in the national newspapers in Ireland, which is rather odd.[23] Whether any offers were made for the estate is not known, as no archival correspondence survived from the above estate agents to throw

The baptistry in All Saints' Church with stained glass windows donated by Bishop Plunket in 1929 and dedicated to deceased members of his family. *Plunket collection.*

any light on the matter. Perhaps Bishop Plunket was only testing the property market at that time and had second thoughts about selling the estate. As it did not sell at that time, it would appear that the comments made by the valuers of the estate almost 20 years previously when Lord Ardilaun died, that 'it would be impossible to find a purchaser for the estate', were proving correct. Perhaps the failure of the estate to sell was due to the fact that all the land was in lease with very high rents, which would not be attractive to buyers. This may have been a factor in Bishop Plunket's decision, over a year later, to acquire the freehold of some of

The Twilight Years

the land. On 17 April 1934, he paid £2,280 to the Vernon and Oulton families, who were then the owners of the Clontarf lands, for the fee simple of the land around the mansion. The amount of land was 47 acres, two roods and eight perches in Heronstown townland, and was the extent of the original Thornhill house and land acquired by the Guinness brothers, Arthur Lee and Benjamin Lee, almost 100 years previously.[24]

The last lavish entertainment held in St Anne's was also the biggest social event seen in Dublin for many years, when Bishop Plunket's daughter Olive married Viscount Milton, son of Lord Fitzwilliam, on 19 April 1933. The wedding took place at St Patrick's Cathedral, Dublin, with Bishop Plunket officiating, and the reception was held in St Anne's. Many people thronged outside the church and at the entrance to St Anne's to watch. A special ship, the 'Lady Connaught', was chartered to bring the tenant farmers and estate workers from the Fitzwilliam estates in England to the wedding in Dublin. A marquee was erected on the lawn of St Anne's to cater for the large crowd, which also included many parishioners from All Saints' Church as well as all the workers on St Anne's estate.[25] Many present-day residents in Clontarf and Raheny have vivid memories of the wedding and have compared the event to 'a Royal wedding.'

The happy couple smilingly acknowledging the cheers of their friends as they left the Cathedral.

The wedding of Olive Plunket and Viscount Milton. *Extract from* Daily Sketch *20 April 1933.*

As mentioned previously, Bedford Lodge had been let to Mary Stapleton for many years, and after her death in 1913 it was vacant for some time. Various tenants occupied the house for the next years and then finally Bishop Plunket leased the house and the caretaker's cottage in the garden to Evelyn C. Penrose, his land agent, for ten years from 1 April 1936, paying the yearly rent of £125.[26]

Bishop Plunket's wife, Dorothea, died on 8 July 1936 and was buried in the only grave in the grounds of All Saints' Church. Lady Ardilaun in her will requested that no graveyard be allowed around the church except for the Plunket family. Bishop Plunket, who had suffered from ill health in later years, was now alone at St Anne's. As his children were either married or working abroad, he was finding the maintenance and upkeep of the house and grounds too much of a burden. The end of an era was now drawing to a close, as maintaining St Anne's as a private house was no longer a viable reality.

CHAPTER TWELVE

Dublin Corporation Years

There seems to be some confusion about exactly how and when Dublin Corporation became involved in acquiring St Anne's. A local community booklet published in 1983 reported that John Keane, the Dublin City Manager, paid a £50 deposit out of his own pocket, without the consent of the Corporation, to the estate agents James H. North for St Anne's estate in November 1936. The following month the Lord Mayor and councillors inspected the property, and at a housing committee meeting shortly afterwards voted to acquire the estate.[1] I am unable to verify the full facts of this report as no record of this housing committee meeting has survived in the archives of Dublin Corporation, and the estate agents James H North lost all their early records in a fire. Some credence to this report was revealed in the *Irish Times* of 5 December 1936, which stated that Dublin Corporation were interested in acquiring land for housing development and among the sites inspected by them was St Anne's estate, which was 'up for disposal for some years past.' The Dublin City Manager reacted to this report in the *Irish Times*, saying it was 'unauthorised and inaccurate.' But the newspaper replied on the 9 December that the only 'inaccuracy' in their report was that the Corporation had actually completed negotiations with Bishop Plunket for the purchase of St Anne's.[2] As Bishop Plunket had been trying to sell the estate since 1932, it is possible that a serious buyer may only have appeared on the scene at the end of 1936, which caused the Dublin City Manager to act quickly.

Regardless of what the accurate sequence of events at that time was, the official Report of the Housing Committee of Dublin Corporation ten years later in 1946 stated that a number of offers were made for the estate at the end of 1936, but the Corporation secured an option to consider all the aspects of the purchase as well as some time to consider the question of acquisition, since they were anxious to acquire land for house building. The property was then valued, but in view of the very wide difference between the price demanded and the valuer's figures, the Corporation later decided to acquire the property by Compulsory Purchase Order (CPO). The Minister of Local Government and Public Health held a local inquiry in relation to the CPO where objections by all interested parties were considered. The Minister finally confirmed the St Anne's Compulsory Purchaser Order 1938, on 8 March 1939. Two agreements, dated 11 July 1938 and 3 August 1939, were signed between Bishop Plunket and Dublin Corporation. Mr George Hewson was appointed sole arbitrator to fix a fair market value, and the total cost of acquisition amounted to £62,000, including the cost of adjustment of boundaries.[3] The Vernon estate's interest in St Anne's was settled before arbitration at £13,862 including costs.[4]

The arbitrator made his award on 1 March 1940. He awarded £18,000 to Bishop Plunket and £21,300 to the Howth estate, as well as compensation to those with leases on the estate. This included Cecil Milne of Maryville (£875), Blayney Hamilton of Bettyville (£950), Arthur Butson of Watermill House (£715), Kathleen Fennell of Watermill cottage (£375) and Teresa Walsh of St Enda's cottage, Watermill Road (£520). The British Legion, Killester received £100 compensation for their yearly tenancy of a field on the Howth Road from the Vernon estate.[5] This was the five-acre field previously mentioned, situated near the entrance to Maryville, which never became part of St Anne's estate. Sometime in the 1920s the Vernon estate finally did rent this field to the British Legion on a yearly tenancy and rent of £20. The field was used for the ex-servicemen's Social Sports Club, which was formed sometime after the Irish Soldiers and Sailors Land Trust built houses nearby at Killester for Irishmen who fought in World War One.[6] All Saints' Church and grounds in Raheny were excluded from the CPO, plus 11 acres of marshland on the coast road at Watermill Road, as well as the tram line along the edge of the estate. The workers on the estate at the time of the CPO who had signed agreements for their houses as part of their employment with Lady Ardilaun or with Bishop Plunket, continued to live and work on the estate. Now they were tenants of Dublin Corporation as well as employees, working as gardeners or caretakers. These workers were as follows:

William O'Keefe signed agreements on 24 March 1915 and 21 May 1926 for the lodge at Sybil Hill, beside the entrance to Vernon Avenue, as caretaker.

Peter Furey occupied the gate lodge on Mount Prospect Avenue, due to his employment on estate, 12 May 1926.

Samuel Corry occupied a cottage on Mount Prospect Avenue, known as Seabank cottage, due to his employment on the estate, 13 May 1926.

Mrs Elizabeth Collins signed as caretaker for a cottage on Watermill Road, Raheny Village, 11 April 1932.

John Brady signed an employment agreement for a gate lodge, known as Ryder's lodge on Mount Prospect Avenue, 29 May 1936.

Thomas McDonnell signed an employment agreement for a cottage on Watermill Road, Raheny Village, vacated by Brady, 1 May 1937.

Thomas Burns was employed as lodge keeper and occupied the gate lodge on the sea road, called Sealawn, 6 December 1937.

James Doran, Sybil Hill, signed as caretaker to occupy the flat of four rooms in the stable yard, 22 June 1938, and agreed not to keep any dogs or fowl in the yard.

Charles McKee of Maryville signed as caretaker for a house and garden called Lilyvale, at Watermill, Raheny, 4 November 1938.

James Doherty signed as caretaker for the house in the garden at St Anne's, 20 May 1940.

Ellen Ryder signed as caretaker for the lodge in the yard at Bedford Lodge, 24 July 1940.

Sybil Hill, home of the Barlow family until added to St Anne's estate in 1876. Became the residence of Bishop Plunket in 1939 and now the residence of the Vincentian Fathers. *J. Sharkey.*

New caretaker agreements were signed by all the above on 3 September 1940, when Dublin Corporation took possession of the estate. This included employing another person, Hugh Savage, as caretaker of the mansion, and he and his family were given three rooms in the mansion.[7]

Sybil Hill house was also excluded from the CPO as Bishop Plunket retained it as his residence with 22 acres of parkland. A boundary wall was built to enclose his new estate at Sybil Hill. In 1938 Bishop Plunket transferred All Saints' Church to the Representative Church Body and also relinquished his right of presentation of the rector, which he had inherited from Lord and Lady Ardilaun. From then on, All Saints' became the parish church of Raheny.[8] On 13 October 1938, Bishop Plunket also sold his lease of Baymount Castle and its 20 acres of land to the new headmaster of Baymount School, John T. Gwynn, for £2,200.[9] The school continued for some years afterwards, but finally closed in 1946. The property was sold to the Jesuit Order, which opened a retreat house, named Manresa, which is still in use today.

While all the negotiations on the CPO were taking place between Bishop Plunket and the Corporation, an auction of the sale of all the furniture and works of art from St Anne's mansion was planned for 9 October 1939. With the outbreak of the Second World War, the auction date was brought forward to 18 September. The year 1939 turned out to be a turning point, not only because of the commencement of the war, but also because all the Guinness houses once owned by Sir Benjamin Lee Guinness – St Anne's, Ashford and the town house at Number 80 St Stephen's Green – all changed ownership in that year.

Early in the year 1939, 22,000 acres of Ashford Castle had been sold by the Iveagh trustees to the State for £20,000 – 10,000 of these acres were placed in the care of the Forestry Services and the remainder was divided up by the Land Commission and sold to tenant farmers. The castle and 100 acres were leased to Noel Huggard, who opened Ashford as a hotel, and it has continued in that capacity, with different owners, up to the present day.[10] On 19 May 1939, Rupert Guinness, the Second Earl of Iveagh, grandson of Sir Benjamin Lee, donated the Guinness town house at St Stephen's Green to the Irish nation, and it was formally accepted by the Taoiseach, Éamon de Valera. The house was officially named Iveagh House by the Government and now serves as the headquarters of the Department of Foreign Affairs.[11] Lastly, Dublin Corporation acquired St Anne's in the same year.

The front page of the *Irish Independent* of Saturday, 6 May 1939, had a full-page advertisement by the auctioneers, Jackson, Stops and McCabe. It announced the upcoming furniture auction at Ashford Castle, Co. Mayo, as well as the announcement of the 'greatest fine art sale ever to be held in Dublin' at St Anne's Clontarf, to be held later in the year. Lord and Lady Ardilaun had been collectors of fine art all their lives and the catalogue for the auction lists a magnificent collection of period furniture, old Waterford glass, books, rare manuscripts, Napoleonic autographs, old silver and oil paintings, as well as the garden statuary and ornaments.[12] The auction at St Anne's opened in the main hall on 18 September and continued for two weeks, attracting large attendance every day. There were over 2,000 lots on offer and high prices were achieved. A fine old Waterford cut-glass chandelier of beautiful design and comprising 24 branches was sold for £200, while a painting, 'The Holy Family with St Elizabeth and St Joseph', attributed to Rubens and from the Blenheim Collection, was sold for £100.[13]

Just as the St Anne's auction was completed, the auction of the contents of Iveagh House, by Messrs Battersby and Company, started on 28 September in the ballroom of the house. Here there were 250 lots on

'The Holy Family with St Elizabeth and St Joseph' attributed to Rubens, sold at St Anne's auction for £100. *Gillman collection.*

Old Waterford cut-glass chandelier sold for £200 at auction. *Gillman collection.*

offer, with many Dublin and London buyers present also.[14] Thus, within a few months of each other, all the fine furniture and painting of the three Guinness houses were sold and scattered. The organ which once graced the drawing room of St Anne's and was admired by Frederick Ogilby in 1840, was moved to the King's Hospital School at Blackhall Place and was later placed in the new chapel when the school moved to Palmerstown in the 1960s.[15] We know the fate of one sculpture. A marble statue of a reclining figure of a shepherd boy, by the Irish sculptor John Hogan, signed and dated 1846, was sold at St Anne's auction to Mr John Burke, a Dublin solicitor, who later presented it to the nation. Today it fittingly rests in the inner hall of Iveagh House, thus connecting the two former Guinness homes.[16]

With the outbreak of war in September 1939, all long-term decisions by Dublin Corporation about St Anne's estate were put on hold. The legal proceedings for possession of the estate by the Corporation were not completed until September 1940, and in the meantime Bishop Plunket let the lands to local farmers, 157 acres being let for the 1940 season. It is interesting to see that the name of the fields in the letting by Bishop Plunket still reflected the former occupiers of over 70 years previously, when his uncle Lord Ardilaun acquired the land, e.g. 'Fottrells, McGowans, Tooles field'. Upon taking possession, the Corporation decided to utilise the land for cultivation purposes. The crop produced enabled the Corporation to make a substantial contribution to the relief of the food situation in the city during the war years. Local people were also given allotments and turf was stacked along the main avenue.

Sadly, a fire broke out in the mansion on 24 December 1943 and it was almost completely destroyed. There was a considerable quantity of air raid precaution (ARP) material belonging to the Department of Defence and the Corporation stored in the house, as well as some items bought by the Corporation at the auction sale. The ARP material included gas masks,

'Shepherd Boy' by John Hogan (1800–1858), formerly part of the Ardilaun collection at St Anne's and now in the hall of Iveagh House. *Department of Foreign Affairs*.

chemicals for decontamination, rubber boots, and clothing. The fire broke out on the second floor and was discovered by the caretaker, Hugh Savage. Firemen assisted by the military, civic guards, Local Defence Force (LDF) and local people, worked to bring the fire, which smouldered for three days under control. A second fire broke out on 27 December but was eventually extinguished. The roof caved in and only the walls of the house remained.[17] A substantial portion of the ARP material was salvaged, while the portion destroyed was covered by insurance, which paid £20,250 for these losses. The mansion was insured by Dublin Corporation for £100,000. There followed much correspondence and many investigations by the insurance company, but the claim was finally settled for the full amount in November 1944.[18] Many local people have always maintained that the fire was malicious, but no written evidence to this effect has been found. Considering that Dublin Corporation initially paid £62,000 for the acquisition of the estate in 1940 and now received £100,000 for fire damage to the mansion, it could be said that the Corporation had made a good profit on their investment.

The lease to the Royal Dublin Golf Club given by Lady Ardilaun in 1919 was now due to expire and Bishop Plunket granted a new lease to the club for 99 years from 1 May 1944 paying a yearly rent of £250.[19] Bishop Plunket spent the last years of his life living at Sybil Hill and regularly attended All Saints' Church, taking a keen interest in all the affairs of the parish. He died on 26 January 1947, and was buried alongside his wife in the only grave in the grounds of All Saints' Church, Raheny. His estate was valued at £40,846 for probate purposes and his younger son Benjamin Plunket inherited Sybil Hill.[20] Benjamin only lived in the house for a few years, and finding it too large, sold both the house and land in 1950 to the Vincentian Fathers. Benjamin Plunket went to live in Delgany, Co. Wicklow, and this move finally broke the Guinness connection with St Anne's estate after 115 years.

This final act was nostalgically marked on 17 February 1951, when Benjamin Plunket, along with other members of his family, formally handed over to the Raheny parishioners the Bishop Plunket Hall to serve as a parochial hall. Mr Plunket said the building had 'a very mixed and

St Anne's: The Story of a Guinness Estate

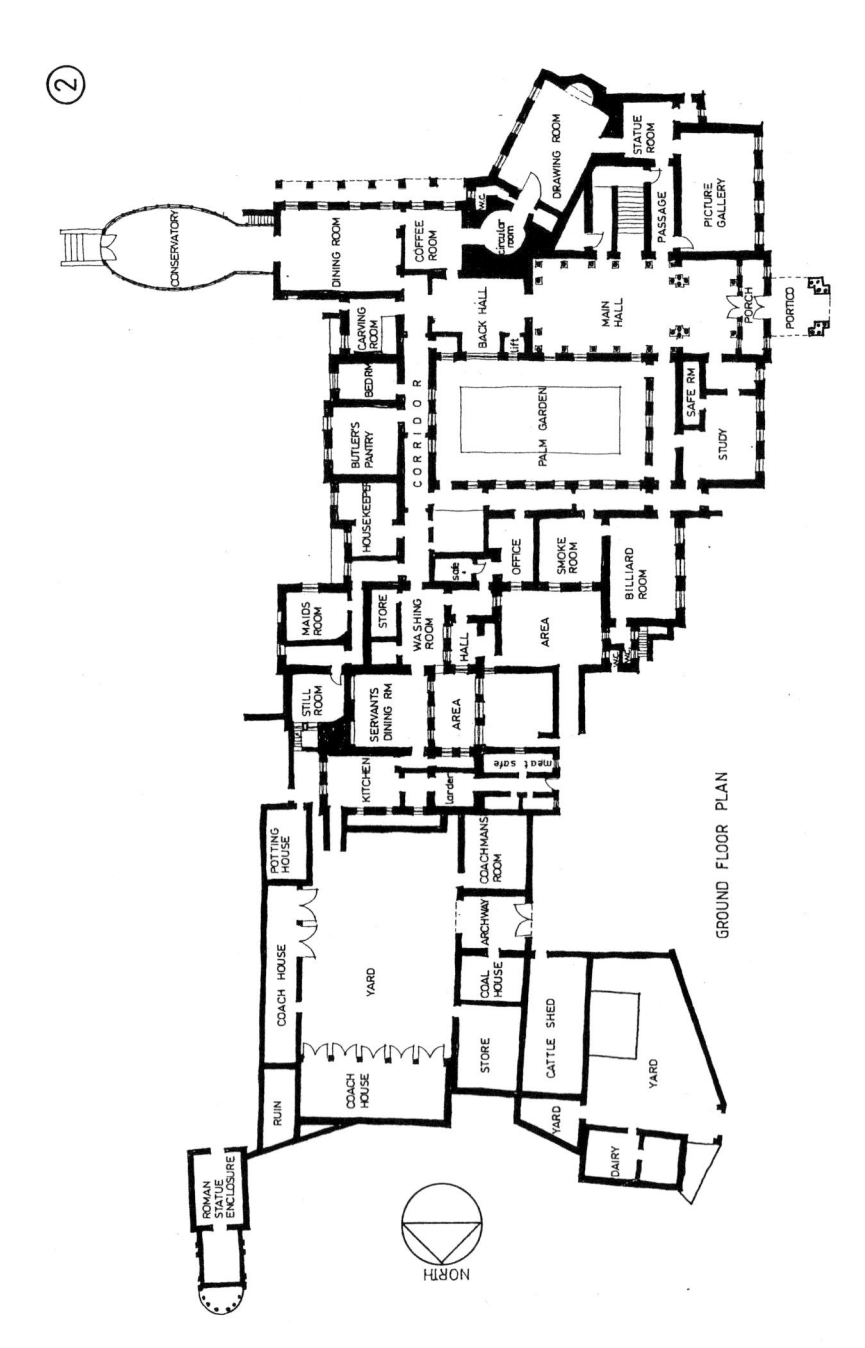

Ground floor plan of St Anne's mansion, surveyed by Housing Architect's Department, Dublin Corporation, October 1941, traced and redrawn later by Leo Devitt.

moving history – physical moving, not emotional' and that he had not looked forward to this day, as it was 'the occasion for me and my family to sever our connection with the parish of Raheny'. Originally Lady Ardilaun built this wooden structure in a field in St Anne's as a pavilion for the Raheny Cricket Club. It was moved to the grounds of the old rectory on the Howth Road when the Corporation acquired St Anne's in 1938 and the cricket club had disbanded. Then Bishop Plunket offered a field in Sybil Hill as a sports ground and the pavilion moved again, to become the social club. Finally, when Benjamin Plunket sold Sybil Hill in 1950, he paid for the removal and re-erection of the pavilion to the grounds of All Saints' Church, to be used as a parochial hall, dedicated to the memory of his late father, Bishop Plunket.[21]

The last connection with the Clontarf and Raheny area was broken on 18 February 1955, when Benjamin Plunket sold the fee simple of North Bull Island to the trustees of the Royal Dublin Golf Club. This included all the land originally conveyed by the Earl of Howth to Lord Ardilaun in July 1894 and also the 922 acres conveyed by the Landed Estates Court to Lord Ardilaun in 1902.[22] Royal Dublin paid £8,500 for the Plunket interest and then sold all the lands outside the club boundary to Dublin Corporation for £12,000. For some years, the Corporation had been in discussions with the Golf Club to acquire the land. A condition of the sale was that the Corporation would erect a fence along the boundary of the links, but this was deferred due to public agitation. Later Royal Dublin released the Corporation from this clause, upon payment of £3,500 to the club.[23] With the acquisition of the recreational amenities available on North Bull Island as well as St Anne's estate, Dublin Corporation had now acquired substantial large tracts of land for the use of the public in north Dublin.

After the war, the Corporation started to make definite plans about the future development of St Anne's estate. About 100 acres was proposed for the building of mostly tenant purchase houses, as well as some private housing on the north side of the estate near to Raheny village. The house building could not start until the Howth Main Drainage Outfall was completed, as Raheny village had no running water. As well as providing sites for schools, two areas were suggested as public playing fields, while the remainder of the estate, circa 230 acres, would be dedicated as a public park. This was the most beautiful area of the estate and included the entire tree-lined main avenue, the pleasure grounds and gardens, together with all the land at the sea front. No decision was made at that time on the future of the burnt mansion and the substantial farm buildings.[24]

The Vernon estate made representations to Dublin Corporation shortly after the CPO was confirmed to buy back two plots of land in St Anne's on the Clontarf side, in order to develop these lands for house-building. The war delayed any progress on these negotiations but finally, in August 1947, three plots of land were sold to the Vernon estate for £8,000. The three plots were: six acres of Sybil Hill townland on Vernon Avenue, two fields of 14 acres in Greenlanes townland on Mount Prospect Avenue, and lastly six acres of the corner site of Heronstown townland, at the corner of Clontarf Road and Mount Prospect Avenue.[25] Private houses were later built on these sites and included the present houses of Vernon Drive, some on Vernon Avenue, all of Baymount Park, Mount Prospect Grove, and some houses on Mount Prospect Avenue and Clontarf Road.

As soon as the Howth Main Drainage was completed, Dublin Corporation commenced their house-building programme in Raheny in 1952, naming the development as the St Anne's Housing Estate. The first families moved into the new houses in 1954. Private houses were also built along the Howth Road and Watermill Road. Many of the old townland names and historical association were kept in the naming of the new roads of the housing estate, e.g. Wade's Avenue, Maryville Road, Naniken Avenue, All Saints' Road, Ballyhoy Avenue. With the increased population, new schools were needed. The new Raheny National School complex, called Scoil Íde, Scoil Assaim and Scoil Áine, was built on All Saints' Drive and opened in 1958, and later a new Garda Station was built opposite the schools to replace the old one in the village. Today this area is home also to many other community groups, including the CARA Community Centre, GAA Club House, Dunseedy Football Club, as well as St Anne's Court, a senior citizens' flat complex. Within a short number of years, the rural village of Raheny had grown to become a suburb of Dublin.

The Vincentian Fathers had been in discussions with Dublin Corporation for some years to acquire a site in St Anne's for a boys' secondary school, and in 1948 the Corporation sold 31 acres in St Anne's estate to them for £9,439. As plans for building the new school took time, the Vincentian Fathers were fortunate that the opportunity to purchase Sybil Hill house and land occured two years later in 1950, when it was offered for sale by Benjamin Plunket. This enabled them to open the new school temporarily in Sybil Hill house. Further discussions between the Vincentian Fathers and Dublin Corporation took place and resulted in three land transactions. In 1952, the Corporation bought back the 31 acres of St Anne's estate from the Vincentian Fathers for £9,938, and then bought 11 acres of the western side of Sybil Hill estate for £8,700. The Vincentian Fathers proceeded with building their new school on the eastern part of the Sybil Hill lands and then purchased an additional 14 acres of St Anne's estate, adjoining the school, to use as playing fields. The Corporation sold this land for £4,200.[26] The new purpose-built school, called St Paul's College, opened later in 1952, and Sybil Hill house became the residence of the priests.

The nearby Maryville house was still occupied by Cecil Milne, who had sub-let some of the rooms in the house to two families. The dairy farm was now gone and Cecil Milne turned the four acres around the house into a market garden for some years. Eventually in 1956 he assigned his lease in Maryville to the Corporation and went to live in Clontarf. Three years later, in 1959, the Corporation sold Maryville house and its four acres to the Vincentian Fathers for £3,500.[27] The house was later demolished and the grounds were used as additional playing fields for the school. Over the following years, with the increased population in the area, St Paul's College expanded with extensions added as well as the building of a swimming pool in 1973. It is now one of the biggest boys' secondary school in the country.

The Corporation had plans to build a new arterial road from Vernon Avenue in Clontarf across the Sybil Hill lands to connect with the Howth Road in Raheny, and to continue over the railway line to Coolock. Shortly after the acquisition of the western part of the Sybil Hill lands in

St Anne's: The Story of a Guinness Estate

Guinness and Plunket Families

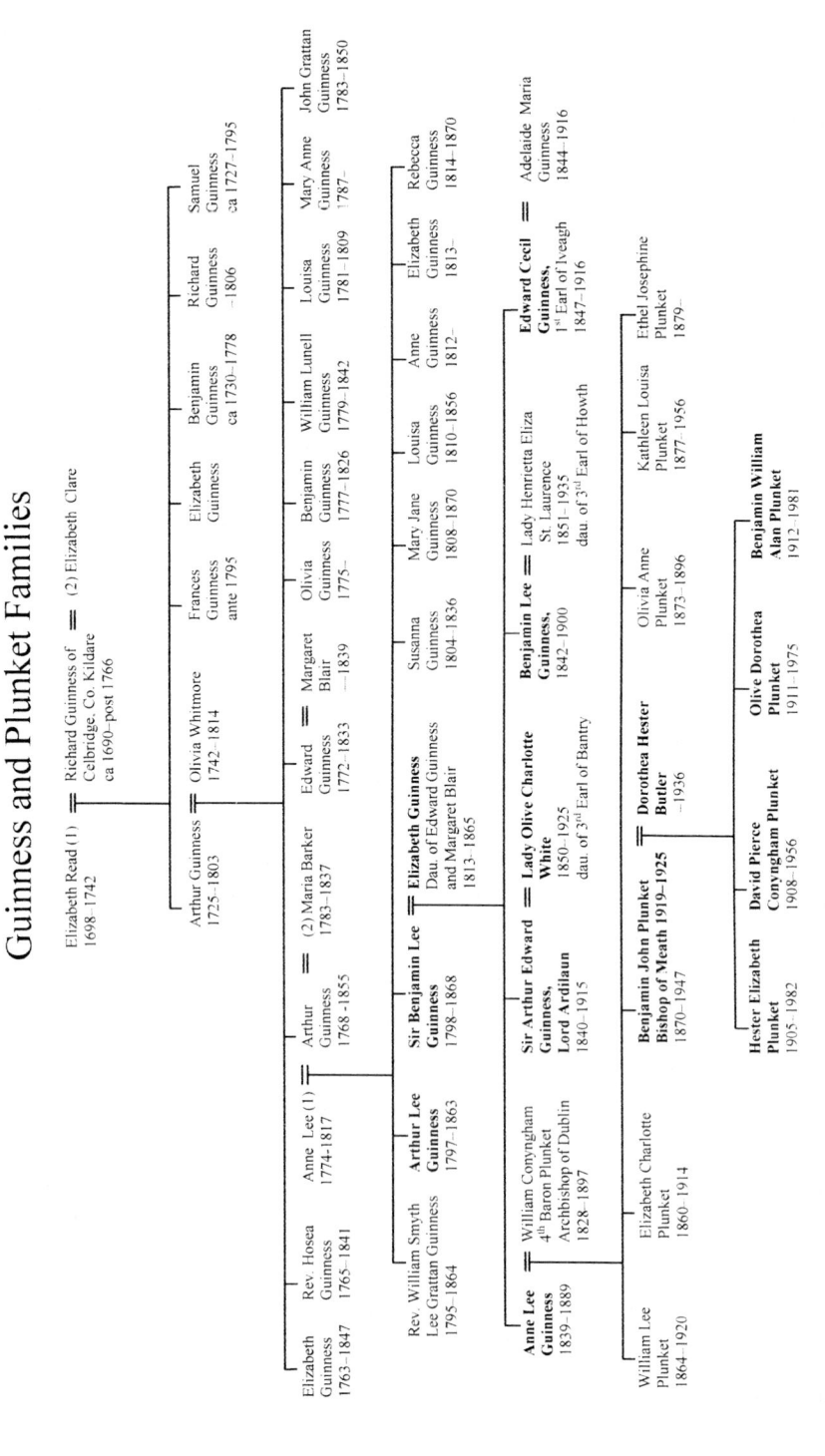

Elizabeth Read (1) 1698–1742 = Richard Guinness of Celbridge, Co. Kildare ca 1690–post 1766 = (2) Elizabeth Clare

Children of Richard Guinness:
- Arthur Guinness 1725–1803 = Olivia Whitmore 1742–1814
- Frances Guinness ante 1795
- Samuel Guinness ca 1727–1795
- Benjamin Guinness ca 1730–1778
- Elizabeth Guinness
- Richard Guinness –1806
- Mary Anne Guinness 1787–
- John Grattan Guinness 1783–1850

Children of Arthur Guinness and Olivia Whitmore:
- Elizabeth Guinness 1763–1847
- Rev. Hosea Guinness 1765–1841
- Arthur Guinness 1768–1855 = Anne Lee (1) 1774–1817 = (2) Maria Barker 1783–1837
- Edward Guinness 1772–1833 = Margaret Blair –1839
- Olivia Guinness 1775–
- Benjamin Guinness 1777–1826
- William Lunell Guinness 1779–1842
- Louisa Guinness 1781–1809

Children of Edward Guinness and Margaret Blair:
- Susanna Guinness 1804–1836
- Mary Jane Guinness 1808–1870
- Louisa Guinness 1810–1856
- Anne Guinness 1812–
- Elizabeth Guinness 1813–
- Rebecca Guinness 1814–1870

Children of Arthur Guinness (1768–1855):
- Rev. William Smyth Lee Grattan Guinness 1795–1864
- Arthur Lee Guinness 1797–1863
- Sir Benjamin Lee Guinness 1798–1868 = Elizabeth Guinness, Dau. of Edward Guinness and Margaret Blair 1813–1865

Children of Sir Benjamin Lee Guinness and Elizabeth Guinness:
- **Anne Lee Guinness** 1839–1889 = William Conyngham 4th Baron Plunket Archbishop of Dublin 1828–1897
- Sir Arthur Edward Guinness, Lord Ardilaun 1840–1915 = Lady Olive Charlotte White 1850–1925, dau. of 3rd Earl of Bantry
- **Benjamin Lee Guinness** 1842–1900 = Lady Henrietta Eliza St. Laurence 1851–1935, dau. of 3rd Earl of Howth
- Edward Cecil Guinness, 1st Earl of Iveagh 1847–1916 = Adelaide Maria Guinness 1844–1916

Children of Anne Lee Guinness and William Conyngham Plunket:
- Elizabeth Guinness Plunket 1864–1847 [sic: 1864–1920]

Children of William Conyngham Plunket:
- William Lee Plunket 1864–1920
- Elizabeth Charlotte Plunket 1860–1914
- **Benjamin John Plunket Bishop of Meath 1919–1925** 1870–1947 ⊨ **Dorothea Hester Butler** –1936
- Ethel Josephine Plunket 1879–

Children of Benjamin John Plunket and Dorothea Hester Butler:
- Hester Elizabeth Plunket 1905–1982
- David Pierce Conyngham Plunket 1908–1956
- Olive Dorothea Plunket 1911–1975
- Benjamin William Alan Plunket 1912–1981

Children of Benjamin Lee Guinness (1842–1900) and Lady Henrietta Eliza St. Laurence:
- Olivia Anne Plunket 1873–1896
- Kathleen Louisa Plunket 1877–1956

Guinness and Plunket Families. Those marked in bold type lived at St Anne's.

1952, the new road was constructed. Initially called Vernon Avenue Extension, it was finally named Sybil Hill Road. The old pedestrian 'right-of-way' tunnel under the main avenue of St Anne's linking Raheny to Clontarf was now no longer needed and was later closed up by Dublin Corporation. Another new road was also constructed along the coast road in 1949 when the tram tracks were removed. Named the James Larkin Road, it also linked the two suburbs and opened up another road to Howth. Later Watermill Road was straightened, which connected with the new causeway road built on North Bull Island in 1964. Providing road access and the increased use of private cars had changed the face of the whole area of this part of north-east Dublin.

The shell of the St Anne's mansion was left derelict after the fire in 1943. In the following years, various proposals were suggested by the Corporation for its future use – as a maternity convalescent home, a sanatorium, a museum or gallery – but none of these were feasible or practicable. Another factor was the cost of restoring the mansion. Left derelict it was vandalised, and with so many young children using the park and playing in the vicinity of the mansion, and the more adventurous climbing into the building, it became dangerous. For safety reasons, it was eventually demolished in July 1968, almost 25 years after the fire, and the headline in the *Evening Herald* recorded it as the 'end of the line for a mansion.'[28] It is sad to reflect that the power of the fire and now the bulldozer had within a short time reduced to rubble all the years of planning and building of this mansion, as well as the enormous expense incurred by both Lord Ardilaun and his father, Sir Benjamin Lee. Today a grassy mound is all that is left to mark the spot.

The fate of other houses and cottages and their occupiers on the estate also changed down through the years. In time, some families left their cottages and moved to the new St Anne's Housing Estate in Raheny. Many of these small cottages and gate lodges were later demolished but some have survived. The attractive gate lodge in the grounds of All Saints' church marks the original Raheny entrance to the estate and became the residence of the sexton of the church. The gate lodge at the original entrance to St Anne's on the James Larkin Road, called Sealawn, is another lovely cottage still in occupation today. Of the original houses on the estate in 1940, five have survived to the present day, i.e. Sybil Hill, Bedford Lodge, and the three red-brick estate cottages on Watermill Road in Raheny village. Those that have gone are Maryville, Bettyville, and the four houses at the junction of Watermill Road and the coast road, namely Watermill House, Watermill bungalow, Lilyvale and Watermill cottage (also called Coragh Cottage). When Blayney Hamilton left Bettyville House, the Local Defence Force used it for the rest of the war years. A family called Simpson occupied a cottage beside Bettyville House for some years but both buildings were later demolished when Watermill Road was straightened. Watermill House and the other nearby cottages were let to tenants for some years, but later they were unoccupied and in time demolished, although their remains can be seen today in the park.

Sybil Hill house is still the residence of the Vincentian Fathers and is one of the oldest of the 'big houses' still standing in the area. It is on the Dublin Corporation's Record of Protected Structures. Further

Bedford Lodge added to St Anne's estate in 1854 by Benjamin Lee Guinness. Later used as the headquarters of the Parks Department of Dublin Corporation for many years, now a private house. *J. Sharkey.*

development of the western side of the Sybil Hill lands occurred over the following years. In 1972 the Little Sisters of the Poor opened the Sacred Heart Home for the elderly, and next to it the Catholic parish of Killester built a new junior boys' school, which opened in 1974. One of the outbuildings of Sybil Hill has also survived and now serves as a community centre for Raheny, Killester and Artane area. After the Penrose family left Bedford Lodge, it was leased to various tenants, including Corporation officials, until 1977. It then became the administrative headquarters of the Parks Department of Dublin Corporation, continuing as such for almost 20 years until the staff moved to the new Civic Offices at Wood Quay in the city. The house was then sold by Dublin Corporation in 1995 and is now a private home. The caretaker's cottage in the grounds of Bedford Lodge had originally been the home of Thomas Ryder, Lady Ardilaun's coachman, and he named it Shellingford. When he died, his family continued to live there and his widow Ellen Ryder, as mentioned previously, was a caretaker first to Bishop Plunket and then to the Corporation. Later it became the home of James Shannon, Superintendent of the Parks Department, whose widow still lives there today.[29]

The three red-brick estate cottages built by Lord Ardilaun on Watermill Road are still intact and mark the former eastern boundary of the estate. The detached cottage used as the Raheny Post Office as well as a residence by Susan Mary Walsh, was called St Enda's. On 18 March 1927, she sold the lease to Mrs Teresa Walsh for £400.[30] Later Mrs Walsh transferred the post office to her own house and shop, 'The Stores', on the Howth Road, where it still serves the local Raheny community today, and is now managed by her grandson, Barry Walsh. Thomas McDonnell and Elizabeth Collins lived in the two semi-detached cottages on Watermill Road when the Corporation acquired St Anne's estate. Their descendants are still living in these two cottages.

The finest architectural inheritance left by Lord Ardilaun to the parish of Raheny is beyond doubt All Saints' Church, which still serves the local Church of Ireland community. In July 1945, the Select Vestry bought a small site beside the church from the Corporation for £140 to build a new rectory. The old Glebe House on the north side of the Howth Road was then sold and later demolished. As already mentioned, when All Saints' Church opened in 1889 it was only dedicated, not consecrated, as the freehold could not be bought at that time. Eventually, in 1969, the Select Vestry bought the freehold from the Howth Estate for £250.[31] Finally, in December 1989, the centenary of the building of the Church, it was consecrated. The church building, boundary wall and gates, as well as some of the interior fittings in the church, are on Dublin Corporation's Record of Protected Structures.

It is now over 60 years since Dublin Corporation acquired St Anne's estate. Although many changes have occurred during this time, the Corporation has achieved the goals it set itself when it first took over the estate in 1940. The compact housing estate of St Anne's, which it built to cater for the housing shortage in Dublin, has developed over the years into a very active and vibrant community. Most of the former demesne and garden of the estate is now a public park and has become a vast recreation area intensively used by the local community as well as serving the wider public of Dublin. Sadly many of the temples and follies have been vandalised over the years, but the legacies of the Ardilauns and their love of trees and gardening have been continued by the Parks and Landscape Services Division of Dublin Corporation. Its central nursery is located in the garden area near the Clock Tower, which produces trees, shrubs, bedding plants and floral tubs for all the city's parks and open spaces. Another legacy are the beautiful Red Stables built by Lord Ardilaun. Used for many years as a machinery depot, with one room used occasionally for exhibitions, plans are presently at an advanced stage for converting them into a centre for visiting artists, where the interesting history of the estate will also be preserved.

The 'jewel in the crown' of the park is undoubtedly St Anne's Rose Garden. The idea for the garden was first promoted by the Clontarf Horticultural Society. The late James Shannon, Parks Superintendent for Dublin Corporation, was responsible for its design. It was officially opened in July 1975 by the Lord Mayor of Dublin and received the Bord Fáilte Civic Award in 1980. Since 1981, it has become a centre for International Rose Trials, making Dublin one of the few cities which holds trials, with the newest unnamed varieties of roses judged by a jury of local and world rose expects each year. Across the main avenue, a miniature rose garden was opened in 1986.[32] To celebrate Dublin's millennium year in 1988, the Parks Department, in co-operation with the Tree Council of Ireland, initiated the Millennium Arboretum. Located north of the main avenue near the St Anne's houses, the area consists of 16 acres planted with over 1,000 different types of trees, and sponsored by 1,000 participants.

Today, the general public is very fortunate in having such a wonderful amenity as St Anne's available to them. With their immense wealth, the Guinness family were able over the years to acquire the land and build up the estate from a mere 50 acres to almost 500 acres. In so doing, they created a beautiful parkland and gardens. They left the public a rich heritage. Their estate was different to many other estates in the country, in that they did not inherit it from the previous generations through confiscation, but acquired it by purchase and through making their fortune in the brewing trade. You could say that life has come full circle for St Anne's estate. The wealth of the Guinness family was built up by the ordinary men and women drinking the famous black porter over the centuries, and today it is they who are reaping the benefits of that wealth.

NOTES TO INTRODUCTION

1   Dublin Corporation, *Dublin City Parks* (Dublin, 1999), pp. 11, 24.

NOTES TO CHAPTER ONE

1   Samuel Lewis, *Topographical Dictionary* (London, 1837), Vol. 1, p. 376.
2   *ibid.*, Vol. 11, p. 481.
3   Francis Elrington Ball, *Howth and its Owners: a History of County Dublin* (Dublin, 1917), pp. 5–6.
4   *ibid.*, pp. 27–28.
5   John D'Alton, *The History of County Dublin* (Dublin, 1838), pp. 55–57.
6   Francis Elrington Ball, *Howth and its Owners*, p. 77.
7   Robert C. Simington, The Civil Survey, AD 1654–56, Vol. VII, County of Dublin (Dublin, 1945), p. 171.
8   John D'Alton, *The History of County Dublin,* pp. 55–57.
9   Dennis McIntyre, *The Meadow of the Bull, A History of Clontarf* (Dublin, 1987), pp. 26–27.
10 *ibid.*, pp. 88–89.

NOTES TO CHAPTER TWO

1   Tony Doohan, *History of Celbridge* (Dublin, n.d.), pp. 43–44.
2   Patrick Lynch & John Vaizey, *Guinness's Brewery in the Irish Economy, 1759–1876* (Cambridge, 1960), p. 69.
3   *ibid.*, p. 70.
4   *ibid.*, p. 74.
5   *ibid.*, pp. 103–104.
6   *ibid.*, p. 105
7   Frederic Mullally, *The Silver Salver: The Story of the Guinness Family* (London, 1981), pp. 18–19.

NOTES TO CHAPTER THREE

1   Registry of Deeds, Book 169, No. 114061.
2   *ibid.*, Book 505, No. 325742.
3   *Saunder's Newsletter & Daily Advertiser,* 19 August 1814.
4   Registry of Deeds, Book 653, No. 455938.
5   *ibid.*, Book 847, No. 567421.
6   *ibid.*, 1835, Book 8, No. 87.
7   *ibid.*, 1835. Book 12, No. 254.
8   *ibid.*, 1835, Book 13, No. 169.
9   *ibid.*, 1835, Book 13, No. 170.

10 *ibid.*, 1836, Book 8, No. 282.
11 *ibid.*, 1838, Book 3, No. 300.
12 Mark Bence-Jones, *A Guide to Irish Country Houses* (London, 1978, Revised Edition 1988), p. 252.
13 Irish Architectural Archives, Ref. No. 2/9/101, Negative, no. S/2328/10.
14 Valuation House Books for Heronstown townland, Clontarf Parish, 1845, p. 24.
15 Edward Malins and Patrick Bowe, *Irish Gardens and Demesnes since 1830* (London, 1980), p. 49.
16 Discussed with Mr David Griffin, Director, Irish Architectural Archives, who agreed with this opinion (February 1998).
17 Michele Guinness, *The Guinness Spirit, Brewers and Bankers, Ministers and Missionaries* (London, 1999), pp. 70–72.
18 Registry of Deeds, 1838, Book 3, No. 300.
19 Patrick Lynch & John Vaizey, *Guinness's Brewery in the Irish Economy, 1759–1876* (Cambridge, 1960), p. 114.
20 Guinness Archives Files, St James's Gate, Dublin. Correspondences on the subject, including research on the history of the miniature obelisk and connection to the original obelisk in Stillorgan Park, by Violet Anderson, Assistant Staff Manager in 1963.

NOTES TO CHAPTER FOUR

1 Valuation Field Book for Civil Parish of Raheny, June 1845, Valuation Office.
2 Registry of Deeds, 1874, Book 4, No. 257.
3 *ibid.*, 1850, Book 8, No. 207.
4 Hodges, Smith & Co., *Survey of Dublin and Meath Estates of Rt. Hon. Earl of Howth* (Privately published, Dublin, 1863), pp. 2, 10.
5 Registry of Deeds, 1854, Book 14, No. 166.
6 Primary Valuation of Tenements, Cancelled Books, Clontarf Parish (1855–1869).
7 Census of Ireland 1871, Table 111, Area, Houses and Population in 1841, 1851, 1861 and 1871 for Heronstown townland, Clontarf Parish, Coolock Barony, County Dublin.
8 Rev. N. Donnelly, D.D., *Short Histories of Dublin Parishes, Part XIV* (Dublin, 1915), p. 31.
9 Primary Valuation of Tenements, Cancelled books, Clontarf Parish (1855–1915).
10 Edward Malins and Patrick Bowe, *Irish Gardens and Demesnes since 1830* (London, 1980), pp. 47–48.
11 Joe Curtis, *Times, Chimes and Charms of Dublin: A Unique Guide to Dublin and its Clocks* (Dublin, 1992), p. 124.
12 Arthur Garrett, *Through Countless Ages: The Story of the Church and Parish of All Saints, Raheny* (Dublin, 1989), pp. 49–50.

NOTES TO CHAPTER FIVE

1. Frederic Mullally, *The Silver Salver: The Story of the Guinness Family* (London, 1981), p. 18.
2. Patrick Lynch & John Vaizey, *Guinness's Brewery in the Irish Economy, 1759–1876* (Cambridge, 1960), p. 214.
3. Registry of Deeds, 1852, Book 18, No. 14.
4. Henry Coulter, *The West of Ireland, Its Existing Condition and Prospects* (Dublin, 1862), pp. 157–158.
5. Representative Church Body Library, Correspondence, Cong, P 38/27; Brigid Clesham, *St Mary's Church Cong, A History* (Cong 1994, Reprinted 1995), pp. 4–5.
6. Registry of Deeds, 1856, Book 13, No. 9.
7. Nicholas Sheaff, *Iveagh House* (Dublin, 1978), pp. 19–21.
8. Lynch and Vaizey, *Guinness's Brewery*, p. 178.
9. *ibid.*, p. 182.
10. *The Dublin Builder,* 1863, Vol. 5, p. 184.
11. Lynch and Vaizey, *Guinness's Brewery*, p. 181.
12. *Irish Times,* 28 May 1868; *Dublin Evening Post,* 28 May 1868.
13. *Irish Builder,* 1875, p. 166, and *ibid.*, 1876, p. 365.
14. Lynch and Vaizey, *Guinness's Brewery*, p. 183.
15. Will Book, 1868, National Archives.
16. Lynch and Vaizey, *Guinness's Brewery*, pp. 182–183.

NOTES TO CHAPTER SIX

1. Frederic Mullally, *The Silver Salver: The Story of the Guinness Family* (London, 1981), p. 27.
2. Marriage Certificate, 16 February 1871, District of Bantry, Union of Bantry, Co. Cork.
3. Mary E. Daly, *Dublin, The Deposed Capital, A Social and Economic History, 1860–1914* (Cork, 1984), pp. 166–167.
4. Arthur Garrett, *Through Countless Ages: The Story of the Church and Parish of All Saints, Raheny* (Dublin, 1989), p. 43.
5. *ibid.*, p. 104.
6. Douglas Appleyard, *In and Out of School, Over two centuries of Coolock and Raheny Schools* (Dublin, 1989), pp. 16–17.
7. *ibid,* pp. 20–23.

NOTES TO CHAPTER SEVEN

1. Registry of Deeds, 1874, Book 4, No. 257.
2. *ibid.*, 1874, Book 26, No. 85.
3. *ibid.*, 1871, Book 8, No. 261.

4   Will Book 1872, National Archives.
5   Registry of Deeds, 1872, Book 37, No. 177.
6   Will Book 1873, National Archives.
7   Primary Valuation, Cancelled Books, Raheny Parish (1868–1883).
8   Registry of Deeds, 1841, Book 11, No. 262.
9   Primary Valuation, Cancelled Books, Raheny Parish (1868–1876).
10 Will Book 1875, National Archives.
11 Primary Valuation, Cancelled Books, Clontarf Parish (1869–76).
12 *ibid.*, Coolock Parish (1855–1890).
13 *ibid.*, Raheny Parish (1868–1883).
14 Death Certificate, 8 February 1880, in the District of Coolock & Drumcondra, Union of North Dublin.
15 Cyril White, 'John Pius Boland: Scholar–Athlete–Statesman and the Establishment of the National University of Ireland', in *UCD Graduates Magazine*, 1984.
16 Registry of Deeds, 1875, Book 46, No. 205.
17 *ibid.*, 1878, Book 47, No. 212.
18 *ibid.*, 1875, Book 51, No. 110.
19 Patrick Lynch & John Vaizey, *Guinness's Brewery in the Irish Economy, 1759–1876* (Cambridge, 1960), pp. 192–194.

NOTES TO CHAPTER EIGHT

1   Will Book 1876, National Archives.
2   Registry of Deeds, 1876, Book 49, No. 188, and Book 74, No. 49927.
3   *ibid.*, 1876, Book 51, No. 131.
4   *ibid.*, 1878, Book 45, No. 153.

NOTES TO CHAPTER NINE

1   Patterson, Kempster & Shortall Collection, 1874–1883, Book 7, p. 375. Irish Architectural Archives.
2   Mark Bence-Jones, *A Guide to Irish Country Houses* (London, 1978, Revised Edition 1988), p. 252.
3   St Anne's Clontarf, Sale Catalogue, 1932, pp. 6–9, National Library.
4   Patterson, Kempston & Shortall Collection, Bills of Quantity for Avenue Tower at St Anne's, February, 1885, Irish Architectural Archives.
5   Edward Malins and Patrick Bowe, *Irish Gardens and Demesnes since 1830* (London, 1980), p. 49.
6   Weston St. John Joyce. *The Neighbourhood of Dublin* (Dublin 1912, Reprinted 1994), p. 253; Katherine Everett, *Bricks and Flowers* (London, 1949, Reprinted 1951), p. 172.
7   Patrick Lynch & John Vaizey, *Guinness's Brewery in the Irish Economy, 1759–1876* (Cambridge, 1960), p. 195.

8   Nicholas Sheaff, *Iveagh House* (Dublin, 1978), p. 23.
9   Frederic Mullally, *The Silver Salver: The Story of the Guinness Family* (London, 1981), p. 28.
10 Ordnance Survey Name Books, Cong Parish, Co. Galway.
11 Nicholas Sheaff, *Iveagh House*, p. 23.
12 Arthur Garrett, *Through Countless Ages: The Story of the Church and Parish of All Saints, Raheny* (Dublin, 1989), p. 49.
13 *ibid.*, p. 154.
14 *The Irish Builder*, 15 May 1886 and 15 July 1891.
15 Arthur Garrett, *Through Countless Ages*, pp. 51–52.
16 Patterson, Kempston & Shortall Collection, Bills of Quantity, December 1884, Irish Architectural Archives; *The Irish Builder*, 15 May 1886.
17 Frederic Mullally, *The Silver Salver*, p. 31.
18 Derek Wilson, *Dark and Light, The Story of the Guinness Family* (London, 1998), p. 111.
19 *ibid.*, p. 116.
20 *Burkes' Peerage, Baronetage & Knightage* (103rd ed., London, 1963), p. 1086.

NOTES TO CHAPTER TEN

1   Olda FitzGerald, *Ashford Castle, Through the Centuries* (Dublin, 2000), pp. 82–87.
2   Gerard Moran, 'Landlord and Tenant Relations in Ireland, Sir Arthur Guinness and his Estate at Ashford Castle, 1868–1882', in *Cathair na Mart* (Vol. 10, No. 1, 1990), pp. 69–78.
3   D.W. Jeffrey, *North Bull Island Dublin Bay – A Modern Coastal Natural History* (Dublin, 1977), p. 117.
4   Registry of Deeds, 1891, Book 24, No. 289.
5   *ibid.*, 1894, Book 50, Nos. 11 and 12.
6   *ibid.*, 1898, Book 27, No. 46.
7   Deed not registered but details of lease given in Probate & Will of Lord Ardilaun, 7 April 1915, National Archives.
8   Registry of Deeds, 1900, Book 83, No. 148.
9   *ibid.*, 1899, Book 84, No. 152.
10 Michael Corcoran, *Through Streets Broad and Narrow, a History of Dublin Trams* (Leicester, 2000), pp. 46–47.
11 *Irish Times*, 20 April 1900.
12 Registry of Deeds, 1902, Book 55, No. 76.
13 *ibid.*, 1903, Book 84, No. 185.
14 Liam Browne & Frank Chambers, *The Royal Dublin Golf Club, 1885–1985, Centenary* (Dublin 1985), p. 27.
15 *Muckross Newsletter*, Issue 8, 1999, p. 8.
16 Derek Wilson, *Dark and Light, The Story of the Guinness Family* (London, 1998), pp. 127–129.

17 *Irish Times,* 21 January 1915.
18 Probate and Will Documents of Lord Ardilaun, Proved 7 April 1915 at Tuam, National Archives.
19 *ibid.,* Valuers' Report, 9 March 1915.

NOTES TO CHAPTER ELEVEN

1   Registry of Deeds, 1920, Book 60, No. 222, and *ibid.* 1925, Book 36, No. 297.
2   *ibid.,* 1932, Book 4, No. 111.
3   Dublin Corporation, St Anne's Compulsory Purchase Order 1938, Leases and correspondence in File No. D 811.
4   Registry of Deeds, 1916, Book 20, No. 286.
5   *ibid.,* 1922, Book 46, No. 92.
6   *ibid.,* 1920, Book 2, No. 192.
7   Dick O'Riordan, *St Anne's Golf Club 1921–1996: a History of the First Seventy Five Years* (Dublin, 1996), pp. 23–25.
8   Liam Browne & Frank Chambers, *The Royal Dublin Golf Club, 1885–1985, Centenary* (Dublin 1985), p. 30.
9   Olda FitzGerald, *Ashford Castle, Through the Centuries* (Dublin, 2000), p. 135.
10 Sean Spellissy, *The History of Galway City and County* (Limerick, 1999), p. 449.
11 Lennox Robinson (ed.), *Lady Gregory's Journals, 1916–1930* (New York, 1947), p. 222.
12 Katherine Everett, *Bricks and Flowers* (London, 1949, Reprinted 1951), pp. 162–164.
13 *ibid.,* pp. 188–192.
14 Arthur Garrett, *Through Countless Ages: The Story of the Church and Parish of All Saints, Raheny* (Dublin, 1989), p. 64.
15 Oral history of Elizabeth Rice McDermott, interviewed by Mary Dunne, Raheny Heritage Society, January 1988; oral history of Theodore Elder in conversation with author, September 1999.
16 Katherine Everett, *Bricks and Flowers,* pp. 179–185.
17 *ibid.,* p. 195.
18 Probate and Will of Lady Ardilaun, 27 January 1926, National Archives.
19 Lennox Robinson (ed.), *Lady Gregory's Journals,* p. 221.
20 Registry of Deeds, 1928, Book 25, No. 36.
21 St Anne's Clontarf, Sale Catalogue, 1932, p. 4, National Library.
22 *ibid.* p. 1.
23 The author checked newspapers for 1931 and 1932 and failed to find any advertisement of the sale. Mr Daniel Gillman has a copy of one advertisement, undated, from an unnamed newspaper.
24 Registry of Deeds 1934, Book 18, No. 10.
25 *Irish Times,* 20 April 1933, pp. 5, 7, 9.
26 St Anne's CPO, Lease in File No. D. 811.

ST ANNE'S: THE STORY OF A GUINNESS ESTATE

NOTES TO CHAPTER TWELVE

1. *St Anne's, Community and Residents' Association Booklet* (Dublin 1983), p. 25. The editor, Edmund Harris, informed the author that he read this account of the acquisition in files held in the office of the Environment Dept. of Dublin Corporation, Wellington Quay, in 1983, but no trace of this file was found when checked by the author in August 1999.
2. *Irish Times,* 5 and 9 December 1936.
3. Minutes of Council Meeting, Dublin Corporation 1939; Dublin Corporation Reports, 1946, No. 28, Report of the Housing Committee.
4. St Anne's CPO, Correspondence in File No. D 814.
5. *ibid.*, Arbitrator's Award, 1 March 1940.
6. *ibid.*, Correspondence in file No. D 814.
7. *ibid.*, Tenant Agreements in file No. D 811.
8. Arthur Garrett, *Through Countless Ages: The Story of the Church and Parish of All Saints, Raheny* (Dublin, 1989), p. 70.
9. Registry of Deeds, 1938, Book 37, No. 108.
10. Olda FitzGerald, *Ashford Castle, Through the Centuries* (Dublin, 2000), p. 140.
11. Nicholas Sheaff, *Iveagh House* (Dublin, 1978), p. 25.
12. St Anne's, Clontarf, Sale Catalogue of the Entire Contents, Jackson, Stops & McCabe, 1939, National Library.
13. *Irish Times,* 21 and 26 September, 1939.
14. *Irish Independent,* 29 September 1939.
15. Arthur Garrett, *Through Countless Ages,* p. 162.
16. Nicholas Sheaff, *Iveagh House,* p. 33.
17. *Irish Times,* 28 December, 1943
18. Dublin Corporation Reports, 1948, Report of the Housing Committee.
19. Registry of Deeds, 1944, Book 15, No. 162
20. Probate and Will of Rev. Benjamin Plunket, 24 March 1947, National Archives.
21. *Raheny Parish Magazine,* April/May 1951, Representative Church Body Library, Dublin.
22. Registry of Deeds, 1955, Book 29, No. 58.
23. Dublin Corporation Reports, 1956, No. 42; *ibid.*, 1957, No. 7; Liam Browne & Frank Chambers, *The Royal Dublin Golf Club, 1885–1985, Centenary* (Dublin 1985), pp. 51–52.
24. Dublin Corporation Reports, 1948, No. 114, Report of the Housing Committee.
25. CPO 1938, Correspondence in File No. D 814: Registry of Deed, 1947, Book 36, No. 299.
26. Dublin Corporation Reports, Report of the Assistant City Manager, 1951, No. 98.
27. Registry of Deeds, 1959, Book 52, No. 56.
28. *Evening Herald,* 25 July 1968.
29. CPO 1938, Housing Rental Record.

30 Registry of Deeds, 1927, Book 10, No. 99.
31 Arthur Garrett, *Through Countless Ages*, p. 80.
32 Dublin Corporation, *The Rose Garden, St Anne's Park, Clontarf, Dublin 3, Silver Jubilee, 1975–2000* (Dublin, 2000), p. 4.

Bibliography

1. Primary Sources.

Census of Ireland 1871, Table III, Area, Houses and Population in 1841, 1851, 1861 and 1871 of each Barony of the County of Dublin.

Census of Ireland 1901, Enumerators' Returns for Raheny and Clontarf Parishes.

Census of Ireland 1911, Emumerators' Returns for Raheny and Clontarf Parishes.

Comparative Abstract of the Population in Ireland 1821 and 1831, County of Dublin.

Cong Church of Ireland, Correspondence, 1860, Representative Church Body Library.

Dublin Corporation, Minutes of the Municipal Council of the City of Dublin. Various years.

Dublin Corporation, Minute Books, General Purposes Committee, Volume I–V, October 1930–April 1945.

Dublin Corporation, Reports and Printed Documents, various years.

Dublin Corporation, Report of Town Planning Department on St Anne's, by C.A. Kelly, 2 July 1957.

Dublin Corporation, St Anne's Compulsory Purchase Order 1938, Original deeds and correspondences in all files held by Muniments Section, Law Department.

Hodges, Smith & Co., Survey of Dublin and Meath Estates of Rt. Hon. Earl of Howth (Privately published, Dublin, 1863).

Ordnance Survey Fair Plan Map, 1837, Parish of Clontarf and Raheny, National Archives.

Ordnance Survey Name Books, County of Dublin, Book 1–4, Typescript, National Library.

Ordnance Survey Name Books, County Galway, Manuscript on microfilm, National Library. Ref. P.2735.

Patterson, Kempster and Shortall Collection, 1874–1893, Irish Architectural Archive.
Primary Valuation of Tenements for the Civil Parish of Clontarf and Raheny, Barony of Coolock, April 1848.
Probate and Will Documents, Lord Ardilaun, 1915, Lady Ardilaun, 1925, and Bishop Plunket, 1947, National Archives.
Raheny Church of Ireland Parish Records, Patents, Deeds, Correspondence, 1796–1976, Representative Church Body Library.
Registry of Deeds, various memorials, 1700–1955.
St Anne's, Clontarf, [Auction] Catalogue of the Entire Contents, Jackson, Stops & McCabe, 9 October 1939, National Library.
St Anne's Sale Catalogue, 1932, National Library.
Tithe Applotment Book for Civil Parish of Clontarf, Dublin, 1829.
Tithe Applotment Book for Civil Parish of Raheny, Co. Dublin, 1830.
Valuation Cancelled Books, 1855–1947, for townlands of Heronstown, Greenlanes, Sybil Hill, North Bull Island & Harmonstown, in Civil Parish of Clontarf, Barony of Coolock.
Valuation Cancelled Books, 1855–1947, for townlands of Bettyville, Charleville, Maryville, Raheny South, Glebe & North Bull Island in Civil Parish of Raheny, Barony of Coolock.
Valuation Field Books for Civil Parish of Raheny, Barony of Coolock, June 1845.
Valuation Field Book for Heronstown townland, Civil Parish of Clontarf, Barony of Coolock, August 1845.
Valuation House Book for Heronstown townland, Civil Parish of Clontarf, 1845.
Valuation House Books for townlands of Bettyville, Maryville & Raheny South, in Civil Parish of Raheny, 1845.
Valuation Office Maps, Sheet 15 and 19, Civil Parish of Clontarf and Raheny.

2. BOOKS

Appleyard, Douglas S., *In and Out of School: Over two Centuries of Coolock and Raheny Schools* (Dublin, 1989).
Ball, Francis Elrington, *Howth and its Owners: A History of Co. Dublin*, Vol. 5. (Dublin 1917, Reprinted 1979).
Begley, Donal F. (ed.), *Irish Genealogy: A Record Finder* (Dublin, 1981).

Bence-Jones, Mark, *A Guide to Irish Country House* (London, 1978, Revised Edition, 1988).
Bence-Jones, Mark, *Twilight of the Ascendency* (London, 1987).
Browne, Liam & Frank Chambers, *The Royal Dublin Golf Club, 1885–1985: Centenary* (Dublin, 1985).
Burke's Peerage Baronetage & Knightage (London, 1963, 103th Edition, 1st Published 1826).
Corcoran, Michael, *Through Streets Broad and Narrow: a History of Dublin Trams* (Leicester, 2000).
Cosgrave, Dillon, *North Dublin City and County* (Dublin 1909, Reprinted 1977).
Coulter, Henry, *The West of Ireland, Its Existing Condition and Prospect* (Dublin, 1862).
Craig, Maurice, *Dublin, 1660–1860: A Social and Architectural History* (Dublin, 1969).
Curtis, Joe, *Times, Chimes and Charms of Dublin: A Unique Guide to Dublin and its Clocks* (Dublin, 1992).
D'Alton, John, *The History of the County of Dublin* (Dublin 1838, Reprinted Cork 1976).
Daly, Mary E, *Dublin: The Deposed Capital, A Social and Economic History 1860–1914* (Cork, 1984).
Doohan, Tony, *History of Celbridge* (Dublin, n.d.).
Everett, Katherine, *Bricks and Flowers* (London, 1949, Reprinted 1951).
Falley, Margaret Dickson, *Irish and Scotch Irish Ancestral Research*, Vol. 1 (USA, 1962).
FitzGerald, Olda, *Ashford Castle: Through the Centuries* (Dublin, 2000).
Garrett, Arthur, *Through Countless Ages: The Story of the Church and Parish of All Saints, Raheny* (Dublin, 1989).
Guinness, Michele, *The Guinness Spirit: Brewers and Bankers, Ministers and Missionaries* (London, 1999).
Howley, James, *The Follies and Garden Buildings of Ireland* (New Haven and London, 1993).
Jeffrey, D.W. *North Bull Island, Dublin Bay, A Modern Coastal Natural History* (Dublin, 1977).
Joyce, St. John Weston, *The Neighbourhood of Dublin* (Dublin, 1912, Reprinted, 1994).
Lewis, Samuel, *A Topographical Dictionary of Ireland*, 2 Vols. (London, 1837).

Lynch, Patrick & John Vaizey, *Guinness's Brewery in the Irish Economy, 1759–1876* (Cambridge, 1960).
Malins, Edward & Patrick Bowe, *Irish Gardens and Demesnes since 1830* (London, 1980).
McIntyre, Dennis, *The Meadow of the Bull: A History of Clontarf* (Dublin, 1987).
Mullally, Frederic, *The Silver Salver: The Story of the Guinness Family* (London, 1981).
Nolan, William, *Tracing the Past: Sources for Local Studies in the Republic of Ireland* (Dublin, 1982).
O'Riordan, Dick, *St Anne's Golf Club 1921–1996: A History of the First Seventy Five Years* (Dublin, 1996).
Pettigrew and Oulton, *Dublin Almanack and General Register of Ireland*, 1834–1847.
Sheaff, Nicholas, *Iveagh House* (Dublin, 1978).
Simington, Robert C., *The Civil Survey, AD 1654–56. Vol. VII, County of Dublin* (Dublin, 1945).
Spellissy, Sean, *The History of Galway City and County* (Limerick, 1999).
Thom's Directory 1844–1904.
Wilson, Derek, *Dark and Light, The Story of the Guinness Family* (London, 1998).

3. JOURNALS/PERIODICALS/BOOKLETS, ETC.

Ashford Castle, Hotel Booklet (Dublin, 1973).
Clesham, Brigid, *St Mary's Church, Cong, A History* (Cong, 1994, Reprinted 1995).
Cong Foroige, Heritage Trail (Cong, 1988).
The Dublin Builder, Vol. 1–8, 1859–1866.
The Irish Builder, Vol. 9–33, 1867–1891.
Dublin City Parks, Map & Guide to Facilities, Dublin Corporation, Parks Department (no date, probably 1988).
Dublin City Parks, Dublin Corporation, Parks and Landscape Services Division (Dublin, 1999).
Muckross Newsletter, Issue 8, 1999, No. 185.
Raheny Parish Magazine, April/May 1951.
Shannon, James, *St Anne's Trail,* Dublin Corporation, Parks Department (no date).

St Anne's, Community and Residents' Association Booklet (Dublin, 1983).
The Rose Garden, St Anne's Park, Clontarf, Dublin 3, Silver Jubilee, 1975–2000 (Dublin, 2000).

Index

Abbey Theatre, 71
Alexandra College, 75
All Saints' Drive, Raheny, 90
All Saints' Road, Raheny, 90
All Saints' Church, Raheny, 51, 52, 61, 65, 66, 71, 73, 74, 76–78, 80, 82, 86, 89, 95, 96
All Saints' Lodge, 93
Allen, Lord, 16
America, 14, 65
Amiens Street, Dublin, 26
Annesley Bridge, 1
Annie Lee tower bridge, 18, 63, 75
Ardilaun Island, 50, 69
Artane, 95
Ashbourne Land Act (1885), 59
Ashford Castle, 57, 58, 74, 83
Ashford estate, 25, 30, 50, 57, 59, 65, 66, 69
Ashlin, George Coppinger, 46, 51, 52
Austrian Pine, 47

Balbriggan, Co. Dublin, 61
Ball family, 11
Ball, Ellen, 11, 17
Ball, Sergeant John, 9, 11
Ball, Mrs, 11
Ball, Reverend Mother, 61
Ballinrobe, Co Mayo, 70
Ballybough, Dublin, 1
Ballyhoy, 37
Ballyhoy Avenue, 90
Bank of Ireland, 7, 20, 35
Bantry, West Cork, 31
Bantry, William, 3rd Earl of, 31
Barlow family, 43, 82
Barlow, James Thomas Barlow, 43
Barlow, John (1746), 43
Barlow, John (magistrate), 43
Barlow, John Herbert Ralph, 43
Battersby and Company, Messrs, 84

Bay of Naples, 21
Baymount Castle, 60, 61, 65–67, 82
Baymount Park, 90
Baymount School, 61, 82
Beaumont Convalescent Home, 6
Beaumont, Co. Dublin, 6
Bedford Lodge, 19, 20, 34, 52, 78, 94, 95
Belcamp, Coolock, 36
Belvidere Terrace, Sandymount, 40
Bence-Jones, Mark, 13
Bettyville, 11, 13, 17–19, 34, 35, 37, 39, 48, 62
Bettyville House (formerly Millbrook Cottage), 39, 75, 80, 94
Black and Tans, 72
Blackbush, 3, 9, 10, 19, 20
Blackbush Lane, 10, 14, 19, 34, 48, 60
Blackwell, Captain John, 3
Blenheim Collection, 84
Boland, Elizabeth, 36, 40, 41
Boland, Mary, 40, 41
Boland, Patrick, 17–19, 35–37, 40
Boland, Patrick, Jnr, 40
Boland's Mills, 40
Bord Fáilte Civic Award, 96
Boru, Brian, 24, 25
Bourn, Mr Bowers, 65
Boycott, Captain Charles, 58
Brady, John, 81
Bricks and Flowers, viii, 70
Brighton Lodge, 36, 39, 48
British Legion, Killester, 80
Buckingham Street, Dublin, 36
Burke, John, 85
Burns, Thomas, 81
Butson, Arthur, 68, 80

Callanan, Reverend James, PP, 20
Campbell, Andrew, 40, 48
Capel Street, Dublin, 17, 40
CARA Community Centre, Raheny, 90

111

Index

Carberry's Brewery, Leixlip, 5
Carlton Terrace, London, 66, 70
Carysfort Avenue, Blackrock, Co. Dublin, 16
Castle, Richard, 27
Castlekirke, Co. Galway, 26
Castleknock, Dublin, 53
Celbridge, Co. Kildare, 5
Celbridge House, 5
Charles II, King, 59
Charleville, 11, 19, 34, 36, 37, 48
Chateau de Malmaison, 48
Christ Church (Priory of Holy Trinity), 2
Church of Ireland, 21, 26, 31, 51, 75, 95
City of Dublin Steam Packet Company, 36
Civic Offices, Wood Quay, Dublin, 95
Civil War, 72
Clare, Elizabeth, 5
Claremorris, Co. Mayo, 70
Clayton, Bishop, 27
Clement III, Pope, 2, 3
Clock Tower, 21, 22, 96
Clonbur, Co. Mayo, 57
Clontarf, xv, xvi, 1, 3, 4, 9–11, 17, 19, 25, 31, 43, 48, 59–63, 77, 89–91, 93
Clontarf and Hill of Howth Tramshed Company Ltd, 62
Clontarf, Battle of, 3
Clontarf Castle, 9, 10, 31, 34, 45, 61, 63
Clontarf Horticultural Society, 96
Clontarf Promenade, xv
Clontarf Road, 63, 90
'Clontarf Sheds', 1, 20
Clontarf Township, 31
Collen Brothers, Messrs, 51, 52
Collins, Elizabeth, 81, 95
Colvill, James, 20
Commissioners of Church Temporalities in Ireland, 41
Compulsory Purchase Order (CPO), 80, 82, 83, 90
Cong Abbey, Co. Mayo, 25, 26
Cong, 26, 57, 59, 70
Connemara, 25, 57

Coolock, 6, 24
Coombe Lying-in-Hospital, 49
Cork, County, 72
Corry, Samuel, 81
Crescent Cottages, Raheny, 32
Cromwell, Oliver, 3
Cusack, Sir Ralph Smith, 48

Daily Express, 65
Darley, Frederick, Alderman, 14,
Darley, Elizabeth (*née* Guinness), 14
Darndale House, Coolock, 39
de Courcey, Sir John, 2
de Lacy family, 2, 3
de Phepo Adam, 3
de Valera, Éamon, 83
Devitt, Leo, 88
Delgany, Co. Wicklow, 86
Department of Foreign Affairs, 26, 83
Dick, Samuel, 32
Doherty, James, 81
Dollymount Beach, xvi
Doran, James, 81
Dublin Ballast Board, 7, 59
Dublin Bay, xv, 2, 3, 14, 21, 46, 47, 59
Dublin Builder, 27
Dublin Castle, 6, 71
Dublin Chamber of Commerce, 7
Dublin City Council, xvi, 10
Dublin Corporation of Brewers, 6, 7
Dublin Corporation, xvi, 14, 50, 79–83, 85–91, 93–96
Dublin Exhibition of Arts and Industries, 27
Dublin Exhibition (1872), 48
Dublin Golf Club, 63
Dublin Mountains, xv, 3
Dublin Port, xv
Dublin, 1, 5–7, 24, 27, 28, 35, 40, 51, 53, 57, 65, 71, 77, 83, 85, 90, 93, 96
Dunseedy Football Club, 90

Easter Rising 1916, 72
Edenmore House, 32
'Eglinton, The', 57

Index

Encumbered Estates Court, 25, 27
England, 7, 75, 77
Espinasse, Paul, 6
Estate Cottages, Watermill Road, 81, 94, 95
Eton College, England, 28, 31
Evening Herald, 93
Evening Mail, 65
Everett, Katherine Olive, viii, 70–72, 75

Famine, The, 16, 25
Farmleigh, 53
Farrell, Thomas, 50
Fennell, Kathleen, 69, 80
Fitzwilliam estates, 77
Fitzwilliam, Lord, 77
Foley, John Henry, 28
Forestry Services, 83
Fottrell, Joseph, 36
Fottrell, Patrick, 35, 36, 86
Fottrell, Walter, 36
Fottrell, William, 36
Fuller, James Franklin, 46, 53
Furey, Peter, 73, 81
Furry Park, 48

GAA Club House, Raheny, 90
Gaisford, Julian, 60
Gaisford-St Lawrence family, 19
Galway, County, 25, 57, 70
Garda Station, Raheny, 90
Gavin Low Ltd., 66
Gladstone's Act of Disestablishment, 31
Glebe House, Raheny Rectory, 2, 32, 89, 95
Glebe land, Raheny, 32, 41, 44
Granby Hill, 60
Grand Canal Street, Dublin, 40
Great Sugar Loaf Mountain, 21
Greenlanes, 34, 90
Gregory, Lady, 71, 75
Guinness family, xvi, 1, 3–5, 7, 27, 28, 50, 92, 97
Guinness Sir Algernon Arthur, 66
Guinness, Adelaide, 53

Guinness, Arthur (*the first*), 5, 6
Guinness, Arthur (*the second*), 7, 8, 24
Guinness, Arthur Francis Benjamin, 3rd Earl of Iveagh, 7
Guinness, Arthur Lee, 8–11, 13, 16, 77
Guinness, Sir Arthur Edward, Lord Ardilaun, 14, 17, 28–37, 39–53, 57–66, 68, 69, 71, 73–76, 82, 83, 86, 89, 93, 95, 96
Guinness, Benjamin, 7
Guinness, Sir Benjamin Lee, 8–11, 13–20, 25–30, 34, 36, 37, 42, 46, 51, 66, 73, 74, 77, 83, 93, 94
Guinness, Capt. Benjamin Lee, 17, 53, 66
Guinness Brewery (*see* St James's Gate)
Guinness, Edward (son of Arthur, *the first*), 13,
Guinness, Edward Cecil, 1st Earl of Iveagh, 17, 28–30, 41, 42, 48, 52, 53, 66
Guinness, Elizabeth (Bessie), 13, 17
Guinness, Reverend Hosea, 7
Guinness, Olive Charlotte, Lady Ardilaun (*née* White), viii, 31, 38, 41, 47, 48, 53, 63, 65, 66, 68–75, 78, 81–83, 86, 89, 95, 96
Guinness, Richard, 5
Guinness, Richard (of Celbridge), 5
Guinness, Rupert, 2nd Earl of Iveagh, 83
Gwynn, John T., 82

Hale, John, 9
Hale, Paul, 9, 10
Hale, William, 9
Hamilton, Blayney, 75, 80, 94
Harden, John, 35, 36
Harmonstown, 44
Harold's Cross, Dublin, 9
Hayes, Reverend Francis, 32
Henry II, King, 2, 3
Herbert Street, Dublin, 37
Herbert, Henry Arthur, 65
Herculanean Temple, 21, 23
Heronstown, 3, 19, 34, 37, 60, 62, 77, 90
Hewson, George, 80

113

INDEX

Hill, Henry, 14
Hogan, John, 85, 86
Holm Oak, 47, 48
Holmes, James Paul, 10
Holmes, John, 9, 10
Holmes, Margaret, 9, 10
Home Rule, 65
House of Lords, 50
Howth, xv, 1, 2, 62, 93
Howth, Christopher, Lord of, 2
Howth, Nicholas, Lord of, 3
Howth, Thomas, 3rd Earl, 17, 18, 34–37, 41, 53, 60
Howth, William Ulick Tristram, 4th Earl, 34–36, 39, 40, 43, 44, 51, 53, 60, 65, 89
Howth Castle, xv, 2, 3, 19
Howth Estate, 19, 80, 96
Howth Head, xv, 3, 60
Howth Main Drainage, 89, 90
Howth Road, 37, 41, 44, 48, 63, 80, 89–91, 95
Howth Survey (1863), 39
Huggard, Noel, 83

International Rose Trials, 96
IRA, 72
Ireland, 7, 25, 75
Irish Architectural Archives, 14
Irish Builder, 51
Irish Free State, 73
Irish Independent, 83
Irish Soldiers and Sailors Land Trust, 80
Irish Times, 63, 65, 66, 79
Italy, 21, 75
Iveagh trustees, 83
Iveagh House (*see* St Stephen's Green)

Jackson, Stops and Joyce, 75
Jackson, Stops and McCabe, 83
James Larkin Road, Dublin, 93
James's Street, Dublin, 6
Jameson, William, 10, 11
Jesuit Order, 83
John, King, 2

Josephine, Empress, 48

Keane, John, 79
Keating, Walter, 44
Kennedy, Ivy, 68
Kennedy, Robert, 68
Kiely, John, 60
Kilbarrack, 36
Kilbarrack Cottage, 60
Killester, 80, 95
Kilmainham, Dublin, 3, 6
Kincaid, Joseph, 18, 19, 35, 37
King's Hospital School, Blackhall Place, 85
Knights Hospitallers, 3
Knights Templar, 3

'Lady Connaught', 77
Lakes of Killarney, 65
Land Commission, 83
Land League, 58, 59, 65
Landed Estates Court, 25, 63, 89
Lee, Anne, 7
Lee, Benjamin, 7, 21, 24
Lee, Rebecca, 7
Leinster Street, Dublin, 18, 37
Leixlip, Co Kildare, 5
Leeson Street, Dublin, 31, 50
Liffey, River, 5
Lilyvale, Watermill, 81, 94
Limerick, County, 72
Little Sisters of the Poor, 95
Little Sugar Loaf Mountain, 21
Lobelia cardinalis, 'The Bishop', 48
Local Defence Force (LDF), 86, 94
London, 7, 28, 53, 65, 85
Loreto, Order of, 60
Lough Corrib, Co Galway, 25, 26, 50
Lough Mask, Co Mayo, 25
Lyon, Alexander, 32

Macroom Castle, Co. Cork, 72, 75
Main Street, Raheny, 40, 69
Manresa, 83
Marsh's Library, 49

Index

Martello Tower, Sutton, 60
Maryville, 34, 36, 43, 66, 68, 80, 81, 91
Maryville House, 43, 44, 68, 80, 91, 94
Maryville Road, 90
Maunsell, John, 32, 33
Mayo, County, 25, 57–59
McDonnell, Thomas, 73, 81, 95
McGowran, Felix, 37, 86
McKee, Charles, 81
Meath, County, 35
Meath Hospital, 6, 7
Millard, Thomas, 13, 14, 46
Millbrook Cottage (*see also* Bettyville House), 37, 39
Millennium Arboretum, 97
Milne, George Cecil, 68, 80, 91
Milton, Viscount, 77
Minister of Local Government and Public Health, 80
Monkstown, Co. Dublin, 37
Montessori School, Raheny, 33
Montgomery, Mary Jane, 68
Moran, Gerald, 58, 59
Morison, William, 3
Morning Mail, 65
Mount Jerome Cemetery, 28
Mount Prospect Avenue, 10, 41, 81, 90
Mount Prospect Grove, 90
Mount Prospect House, 34
Mountjoy Square, North, 1
Muckross Estate, Co. Kerry, 65
Mulally, Frederic, 5
Mulock, Catherine, 10
Mulock, William Henry, 10, 11
Murphy, Timothy and Sons, Messrs, 26

Naniken Avenue, 90
Naniken River, 3, 13, 21, 60, 62
National Library of Ireland, 75
Newbold, Colonel Charles, 75
Nixon, James, 20
North Bull Island, xv, xvi, 59, 60, 62, 63, 65–67, 69, 89, 93
North Bull Wall, xv, 59
North Strand, 1

North, James H., 75, 79

O'Hanlon, Jane, 69
O'Keefe, William, 81
O'Reilly family, 9
O'Reilly, Fleming, 1
O'Reilly, Hugh, 1, 10
O'Rourke, Patrick, 37
O'Toole, Anthony, 35, 37, 39, 40, 57, 86
O'Toole, Denis, 39
Oakley Park, Co Kildare, 5
Ogilby, Elizabeth (*née* Darley), 14
Ogilby, Frederick Darley, 14, 46, 85
Oranmore and Browne, Lord, 25
Oughterard, Co. Kildare, 6
Oulton family, 77

Palmerstown, Co. Dublin, 85
Paris, 11
Parks & Landscape Services Division, Dublin Corporation, xvi, 94–97
Pearce, Sir Edward Levett, 16
Penrose, Evelyn C., 78, 95
Phoenix Park, 53, 63
Pim's Mills, 40
Plunket, Anne Lee, Lady (*née* Guinness), 17, 18, 28, 51, 73, 75
Plunket Hall, Bishop, 86, 89
Plunket, Benjamin, 86, 89, 91
Plunket, Dorothea, 78
Plunket family, 92
Plunket, Olive, 77
Plunket, Reverend Benjamin John, Bishop of Meath, 48, 73, 74, 76–83, 85, 86, 89, 95
Plunket, William Cunningham, 4th Baron, Archbishop of Dublin, 28, 51, 73
Plunkett, Elizabeth, 3
Pompeian Temple, 21, 23
Portadown, Co. Down, 51
Price, Reverend Dr Arthur, Archbishop of Cashel, 5
Prince of Wales (later King Edward VII), 27, 38, 53
Prince of Wales (later King George V), 57

Index

Princess of Wales, 53
Purser, John, Jnr, 8, 24

Raheny, xv, xvi, 1–4, 9, 11, 13, 17–19, 21, 31, 32, 34–37, 39–41, 43, 44, 48, 50, 51, 59, 60, 69, 72, 77, 80–82, 87, 89–91, 93, 95
Raheny Cottage, 11
Raheny Cricket Club, 89
Raheny Infant School, 21, 32, 33
Raheny Park, 40
Raheny Parochial School, 32, 33, 69
Raheny Post Office (St Enda's), 69, 80, 95
Raheny Select Vestry, 21, 32, 72, 95, 96
Raheny South, 18, 19, 34, 37, 40, 48
Rainsford family, 6
Rainsford Street, 6
Read, Elizabeth, 5
Record of Protected Structures, Dublin Corporation, 94, 96
Red Stables, 52, 96
Representative Body of the Church of Ireland, 32, 35, 43, 60, 82
Roman Tomb of the Julii, 12, 14, 15, 47
Rose Garden, St Anne's Park, xvi, 48, 96
Royal Dublin Golf Club, xvi, 63, 69, 86, 89
Royal Dublin Society, 49
Royal Navy, 61
Rubens, 84
Ryder, Ellen, 81, 95
Ryder, Thomas, 95
Ryder's Lodge, 81

Sacred Heart Home, Sybil Hill, 95
Sacred Heart Order, 50
Salisbury Cathedral, 51
Santry River, 62
Savage, Hugh, 82, 86
Scoil Áine, 90
Scoil Assaim, 90
Scoil Íde, 90
Scotland, 7
Scott, William Lucas, 61
Seabank Cottage, 81

Sealawn Cottage, 81, 93
Seapark House, 34
Shannon, James, 95, 96
Shelbourne Hotel, 71
Shellingford, 78, 81, 95
'Shepherd Boy', 85, 86
Silver Salver, The, 5
Simpson Family, 94
Sinn Féin, 71
Sisters of Charity, 6
Slade School, London, 71
Slater's Directory, 39
Snug townland, 37
Social Sports Club, 80
South Wall, 'The Piles', xv
'Souvenir de la Malmaison', 48
'Souvenir de St Anne's', 48
St Ann's, 13, 14, 46, 55
St Ann's Well, 13, 14
St Anne's, xvi, 5, 8, 14, 16, 17, 19–21, 25, 28–31, 33–37, 39–41, 43–52, 57, 59, 60, 62–68, 70–75, 77–85, 87, 89–97
St Anne's Court, 90
St Anne's Golf Club, xvi, 69
St Annes' House, 47, 49, 50–52, 54–56, 70, 71, 73, 74, 83–86, 88, 93
St Anne's Housing Estate, 90, 93, 96, 97
St Anne's Regional Park, xvi
St Assam's Church of Ireland, Raheny, 32, 50, 51
St Doulough's, Balgriffin, 36
St Enda's (*see* Raheny Post Office)
St James's Gate (Guinness Brewery), 5–7, 16, 24, 28, 75
St Lawrence family, 2–4
St Lawrence, Lady Henrietta, 53
St Mary's Abbey, Dublin, 2
St Mary's Church, Cong, Co. Mayo, 26
St Patrick's Cathedral, 6, 27, 28, 49, 77
St Paul's College, 91
St Rémy, France, 14
St Stephen's Green, 49, 50
St Stephen's Green (No. 42, Lady Ardilaun's town house), 66, 71, 73

116

INDEX

St. Stephen's Green (No. 80/81, Iveagh House), 26, 30, 53, 83–86
St Stephen's Green (Dublin) Act, 49
St Werburgh's, Dublin, 7
Stapleton, Mary, 20, 34, 78
Stapleton, Sarah, 20
Station House, Raheny, 37
Station Road, Raheny, 21
Stillorgan Park, Co. Dublin, 16
Stopford & Turner, Messrs, 66, 67
'Stores, The', 95
Strongbow, Earl of, 2
Sunday School, 6
Sutton, xv, 63
Sybil Hill, 41, 43, 61, 63, 81, 89–91, 95
Sybil Hill House, 44, 48, 70, 72, 75, 82, 86, 91, 94
Sybil Hill Road, 93

Thomas Street, Dublin, 9, 25, 27
Thornhill, 3, 9–11, 13, 14, 46, 77
Tickell, Adelaide, 61
Tickell, George, 61
Tolka River, 1
Thom's Directory, 17, 36, 39, 44
Trail, Doctor, Bishop of Down and Connor, 60
Tree Council of Ireland, 97
Trinity College, Dublin, 25, 28, 31
Tristram, Almeric (*the first*), 2
Tristram, Almeric (*the second*), 2
Tristram, Nicholas, 2
Tuam, Bishop of, 26

Ulster, 2
United Kingdom, 24
Upper Meadow, Blackbush, 10

Vanderbilts, 46
Vernon Avenue, 61, 81, 90, 91
Vernon Avenue Extension, 93
Vernon Drive, 90

Vernon family, 2–4, 45, 59, 60, 65, 77, 80, 90
Vernon, Edward, 61, 63
Vernon, John Edward Venables, 3, 10, 11, 13, 19, 20, 31
Vernon, John (1640), 3
Vernon, John (1747), 9, 10, 43
Victoria, Queen, 63
'Village House', Raheny, 69
Vincent family, 65
Vincent, Maud, 65
Vincentian Fathers, 82, 86, 91, 94
Violet Hill, 32

Wade, Sarah, 37
Wade's Avenue, 90
Wade's Lane, 48
Walker, John J., 20
Walsh, Barry, 95
Walsh, Susan Mary, 69, 95
Walsh, Teresa, 80, 95
Warren, Robert, 60
Waterford Glass, 83–85
Waterloo, Battle of, 8
Watermill Cottage/Bungalow (thatched), 68, 69
Watermill Cottage (Corragh/Strand Cottage), 68, 69, 80, 94
Watermill House, 17, 19, 35–37, 39, 40, 68, 69, 80, 94
Watermill Road, 40, 41, 48, 69, 80, 81, 90, 93, 94
Weekly Warden, 65
Westminster, 49
Whitmore, Olivia, 6
Wicklow Mountains, xv, 3
Winton House, Leeson St., 40
World War One, 69, 80
World War Two, 83, 85

Yew Garden, 21, 22, 74